11-18-68

THE PSYCHOLOGY
of DISCIPLINE
in the CLASSROOM

THE PSYCHOLOGY

of DISCIPLINE

in the CLASSROOM

William J. Gnagey

PROFESSOR OF PSYCHOLOGY
ILLINOIS STATE UNIVERSITY

THE MACMILLAN COMPANY, NEW YORK
COLLIER-MACMILLAN LIMITED, LONDON

Second Printing, 1968

Library of Congress catalog card number: 68–11859

THE MACMILLAN COMPANY, NEW YORK
COLLIER-MACMILLAN CANADA, LTD., TORONTO, ONTARIO

Printed in the United States of America

Preface

T HIS BOOK IS AN ATTEMPT to bring together the colorful and exciting adventure of classroom teaching and the precise statistical operation of the research scientist. Its goal is to illustrate the latest findings in discipline research with authentic incidents from living, breathing classroom situations.

One purpose of such a venture is to provide the classroom teacher with a versatile tool for helping deviant students become more efficient learners. Perhaps some teachers will use the book as a shield against the onslaught of disciplinary chaos.

In Chapter 1, the five components of a deviancy episode appear in a roistering classroom disaster that highlights their dynamic interaction.

Chapters 2 through 6 focus on these essential aspects, bringing the results of clinical and experimental research to bear on each one in turn.

In Chapter 7, a psychological model of deviancy control is employed to organize and facilitate the application of the material in the preceding chapters.

The final chapter describes and analyzes five case studies in which the psychological model was systematically applied with gratifying results.

It is hoped that *The Psychology of Discipline in the Classroom* will prove to be an enjoyable and enlightening piece of professional literature that can stand up under the rigors of the academic firing line.

W. J. G.

Normal, Illinois

Contents

1

The Deviancy Episode:
An Introduction

MR. LINKER had just left the room to answer an emergency telephone call in the principal's office. His freshman algebra class was supposed to be starting their next day's assignment. Although he hadn't had time to explain the lesson fully, he had instructed the group to get down to work while he was gone and warned them that there was to be no "funny business" while he was away.

Things went all right for nearly ten minutes. By this time about two-thirds of the class seemed to be hung up on problem three. There was some discussion about a new term, and several of the conscientious members of the class approached Ronald about the matter. Ronald, an "A" student, was already on number five and didn't want to be bothered. The buzzing increased in volume, and some giggling began in one corner.

It was at this point that Roscoe began his little act. Pulling his glasses down on his nose like the principal, Mr. Beggs, he began an artful and uproarious takeoff on a recent auditorium harangue that Mr. Beggs had made, concerning the proper clothing to be worn at Streamline High. The class was immediately convulsed and showed their appreciation with uncontrolled laughter and a few boos and catcalls. This response spurred Roscoe on to even greater heights.

No one knew how long Mr. Beggs had been peering through the window, but everyone knew Mr. Beggs was furious. Tight-lipped and white with anger, the principal intruded into the

1

bedlam at the peak of Roscoe's mimicry. The program ground to an ominous halt.

The principal shoved Roscoe roughly against the front wall and began the inevitable reprimand. "I might have known it would be you, Roscoe," he seethed. "You've been accomplishing nothing but this asinine clowning ever since you came here. And look at your clothes! Blue jeans and a sweatshirt! It certainly proves what I was saying the other day in the auditorium: Sloppy dress goes with a sloppy learner. But this time you won't get away with it. Get down to my office and we'll see how funny you feel when you're parents find out that you're expelled for a month."

Mr. Beggs thrust Roscoe toward the door and turned to glare at the class. "Since you all thought the little act was so funny, you can report to this room after school for a forty-minute detention period. Mr. Linker will be here to see that no more of this buffoonery goes on." This last pronouncement was shot at the returning algebra teacher who had just re-entered the room.

Mr. Beggs made a stormy exit hauling the hapless Roscoe forcefully by one arm. Mr. Linker closed the door quietly as he tried to imagine how such a volcano could have erupted in fifteen short minutes.

How Can You Stop a Volcano from Erupting?

It is the rare teacher who hasn't had something like this happen to his class. The names and faces may be different, but the plot is all too familiar. Somehow things get out of hand, and the roof blows off, and you wonder how you ever got into such a fix.

It's enough of a disaster to your self-confidence when the explosion can be contained within your own classroom, but when your principal gets into the act, small feelings of anxiety begin to well-up inside you. You know too well that more teachers are fired for their inability to keep discipline than for any other reason. Something has got to change!

The problem is deciding where to begin. Your college courses —what you can remember of them—all seem so general. There were no Roscoes or Ronalds or Mr. Beggses in the educational psychology text, but your instructor is certain to have made some pointed allegations about how most discipline problems are traceable to some weakness in the teaching. Your anxiety feelings begin to border on panic.

Certainly this is an appropriate place at which to bring some order out of the chaos.

ANALYZE THE MISBEHAVIOR SITUATION

Jacob Kounin and his associates (1961) have devised a model by which most misbehavior situations can be readily analyzed. Within each disciplinary incident, we can quickly distinguish the following aspects: the deviancy, the deviant, the teacher, the control technique, and the audience.

The term *deviancy* refers to the misbehavior itself. Depending on the rules that Mr. Linker had set up in his algebra class, there may have been several deviancies in our opening example. If talking to other students without permission was forbidden, then every person who went to Ronald for help was committing a deviancy. If giggling and buzzing were taboo in Mr. Linker's room, then at least two other deviancies should be added to the list. Perhaps the most obvious deviancy was Roscoe's irreverent portrayal of his principal, but, as far as Mr. Beggs was concerned, enjoying it was almost as bad. In any case, in this model, all misbehaviors are called deviancies.

A *deviant* is the person who misbehaves. It makes no difference whether he is a chronic defendant or whether it is his first offense: If he breaks a rule of the classroom, he is called a deviant in that situation. Of course Roscoe emerges as the arch-deviant in our classroom drama, but under the proper circumstances, almost every student in the class may have been a deviant before the last act was finished.

Perhaps the *teacher* should have been listed as the first part of the model since it is from his side of the desk that this book is written. In the discipline episode, however, the teacher usually enters the picture after a deviant has performed the deviancy, and that is why we mention him at this point in the sequence. Although Mr. Linker would ordinarily be thought of as the teacher in our example, closer scrutiny makes it obvious that as far as the misbehavior episode was concerned, the principal fits more properly into this category.

The teacher's usual function in the disciplinary episode is to perform some *control technique*. Any action that he takes to stop a deviant from misbehaving or to prevent a deviancy from recurring may be called a control technique. Although Mr. Linker made some attempt to forestall deviancies in his absence by warning against "funny business," the important control techniques in this episode were performed by Mr. Beggs. Such acts as shoving Roscoe against the wall, berating his behavior and his dress, threatening to expel the boy from school, sentencing the class to a forty-minute detention period, and hauling Roscoe off to the office are all properly categorized as control techniques.

The *audience* is just another term for the classmates of the deviant who are witness to, but not targets of, all the control techniques. We will be especially interested in their reaction to the teacher's attempts to control the deviant. As you know, giant eruptions from little tremors grow.

APPLY THE RESULTS OF RESEARCH

In the remaining chapters of this book, we will take up each aspect of the discipline model in more detail. In each case we will try to emphasize material from experimental and clinical research that will be directly applicable to discipline problems that are common in the public-school classroom.

It is our hope that each chapter will help your panic to subside and allow you to gain more expertise in the prevention and control of serious disciplinary eruptions.

References

Kounin, J. S., P. V. Gump, and J. Ryan. Explorations in classroom management. *Journal of Teacher Education*, 1961, *12*, 235–246.

2

Deviancy: When Behavior
Is Misbehavior

A SECOND-GRADER recently took it upon himself to educate me about some of the facts of school life. I had merely asked him how his gym class was going and was unprepared for the lecture that followed.

"Just great!" he said. "Ever since Miss Brinker came, I really like gym. When Miss Crane used to teach us, she yelled at us all the time. We couldn't have any fun. But Miss Brinker doesn't care if you have a little fun. She is a beautiful teacher!"

Although I would certainly be unwilling to base a serious evaluation on the Misses Brinker and Crane on the exuberant statements of one small lad, he does make one important point without really meaning to: *What is misbehavior to some teachers is certainly not to others.* This chapter attempts to define misbehavior and describe several bases for judging an act to be deviant.

WHAT IS MISBEHAVIOR?

Someone has pointed out that a weed is any plant that grows where it is not wanted. A hybrid corn plant is just as much a weed in a flowerbed as a morning glory in a cornfield. The classification of a plant as a weed is much more dependent upon the purposes of the gardener than upon any characteristic of the plant itself.

Our definition of misbehavior draws a close parallel to the one above: Misbehavior is any action that is taken where it is not

5

wanted. A quiet, business-like demeanor at a party may be just as out of place as a gay, frolicsome approach to long division. The appropriateness of behavior is much more dependent upon the purposes of the teacher than upon any characteristic of the behavior itself.

In some high schools, appearing "grubby" at school (dungarees and a sweatshirt) is considered a misdemeanor, although in other locales this is the accepted modal attire. In some sections of a city, a boy may carry a pocketknife to school without ever being questioned. In other schools in the same city, even nail files are confiscated as potentially dangerous weapons.

Situations like these have convinced us that it is a fruitless approach to attempt to categorize misbehavior in terms of the responses themselves. We believe that the only realistic postion one can take is that any behavior is deviant if the teacher (principal, school board) deems it so.

WHAT ARE SOME DEVIANCIES TEACHERS LIST?

Even with our admission that a deviancy is what the teacher says it is, it is amusing, if not instructive to look at some lists of misbehaviors that have been compiled over the last one hundred years or so in this country. S. L. Pressey (1939) found a list of deviancies published by a North Carolina high school in 1848. Here are some of them arranged in descending order of seriousness:

1. Playing cards at school (10 lashes)
2. Swearing at school (8 lashes)
3. Drinking liquor at school (8 lashes)
4. Telling lies (7 lashes)
5. Boys and girls playing together (4 lashes)
6. Quarreling (4 lashes)
7. Wearing long fingernails (2 lashes)
8. Blotting one's copybook (2 lashes)
9. Neglecting to bow when going home (2 lashes)

The *Elementary School Journal* for October, 1928, carried a list of offenses together with the punishments thought appropriate for each. Some of the items on H. W. James' list follow:

1. Truancy
   a. Keep pupil in after school to make up work
   b. Report case to parents
   c. Report case to public officer
2. The "show-off" attitude
   a. Put offender in place by a remark that will enlist pupils on your side
   b. Removal of privileges
   c. Public acknowledgment of fault
3. Dishonesty in assigned work
   a. Removal of credit
   b. Assignment of extra work
   c. Seat pupil apart from the group
4. Overzealousness in recitation
   a. Assignment of extra work
5. Bullying
   a. Oral reproof
   b. Removal of privileges

When Schrupp and Gjerde (1953) asked teachers to rate student behaviors which they currently considered to be serious, the following partial list emerged: defiance, rudeness, obscene notes and pictures, disobedience, disorderliness, heterosexual activity, masturbation, and untruthfulness.

J. E. Greene (1962) compiled the following array of alleged misbehaviors cited by the teachers of senior-high-school students. They are listed in order of their frequency: talking, disobedience, carelessness, defiance of authority, cutting class, inattention, tardiness, cheating, and throwing objects.

WHAT INFLUENCES A TEACHER'S JUDGMENTS OF DEVIANCY?

A glance at these lists of misbehaviors and a quick perusal of your own experiences will attest to the fact that even though judgments may change with time and place, there are some startling similarities among the arrays of discipline problems teachers encounter in their professional careers. You may remember being considerably relieved the first time you found out that other teachers (and many of them experienced) were having the same kinds of disciplinary problems that you were. Suddenly you were not alone anymore but one of the ranks of the battle-scarred veterans who daily braved the disciplinary challenges of public-school classrooms.

One way of organizing this plethora of alleged offenses consists of placing each deviancy in one of five different categories. These categories are based on the type of consideration a teacher makes when he judges any action to be deviant.

Moral considerations seem to be one major influence underlying the deviancy judgments expressed on the lists we have presented. At least nine of the misbehaviors listed earlier were probably judged so on the basis of their moral implications. Playing cards, swearing, drinking, lying, long fingernails, heterosexual activity, obscenity, and masturbation were all probably considered immoral by the teachers who listed them. The fact that "boys and girls playing together" was deserving of four lashes in 1848 is a startling reminder that we are forever operating under a "new morality." Unless a teacher wishes to run the risk of imposing his own ethics upon the children of citizens who also have freedom of belief, he must constantly be looking for a more inclusive standard.

Though the specific items on the list may change from one time or locale to another, moral implications of behavior will no doubt remain a potent influence on teachers' disciplinary decisions.

Personal considerations also seem to have influenced a great many of the deviancy judgments we have cited. Although all evaluations may be thought of as somewhat personal, this category is reserved for those behaviors which irk the teacher for reasons of preference unique to himself. Failure to bow, a "show-off" attitude, overzealousness in recitation, carelessness, defiance, rudeness, and disobedience all show a strong personal element behind their indictment.

Legal considerations could include both those prohibitions that are part of the state or local school law and extra-legal rules made by the administrative personnel of a building. Truancy, cutting class, and tardiness probably fall into this category.

Incidentally, a great deal of conflict can arise when the prohibitions thought important by the principal are not judged important by his staff. A teacher's decision to ignore an administrative "gum-chewing" or "no-Levis" rule is fraught with all kinds of anxiety-producing ingredients.

Saftey considerations will almost certainly overlap the legal and moral aspects of judgment, but there may be some behaviors that are taboo principally because of their threat to the health and safety of the students. Quarreling, bullying, and throwing objects could easily fit into this category. With the advent of the high-school automobile operator, drinking could be placed here also. One could realistically add the fire hazard of smoking to the list.

Educational considerations make up the last of the elements of our model. Only a few of the twenty-eight deviancies on our lists fell clearly into this category, although several others might have shared this designation with another. Inattention and talking would certainly impede the learning process, while cheating, tardiness, and truancy could be objected to on educational grounds. As with most human judgments, almost every misdeed cited could be censured for a number of reasons.

How Can Your List of Rules Be Improved?

Since misbehavior is defined by the classroom teacher, the composition of his private list of rules is of primary importance. One experimenter (Crispin, 1966) has shown that a teacher tends to use the same proportion of disciplinary actions regardless of the class or the subject matter.

This might indicate that once a teacher forms a list of rules he tends to enforce them day after day and class after class. If this is true, one way to decrease the number of deviancies might be to form a new list.

MAKE THE LIST MINIMAL

The recreation staff at Middle State Orphanage were at their wits' end. The weekly dance held for their teen-aged charges had become a nightmare of delinquency. Both fellows and girls seemed bent on coming to the dance in the grubbiest attire that they could find. Determined to teach them something about proper dress, the recreation leaders spent the better part of each evening insisting that the boys tuck in their shirts and that the girls must wear skirts instead of pants. Their demands were met with hostility and defiance, and the dances were hardly worth holding.

In consultation with a local psychologist, the staff decided that their grooming demands were a lot less important than the wholesome recreation they were trying to provide. They reasoned that adolescents in a state orphanage had already had more than their share of frustrations and that adding new ones should only be done where absolutely essential.

For the next month, nothing was said about shirt tails or skirts during the weekly recreation dances. Not only was the staff relieved of the necessity of spending all evening as policemen, but incidents resulting from student hostility at the rules disappeared. Several months later the group reported to the psychologist that the dances were going smoothly and the level of dress had slowly improved.

This is just one example of a situation in which teachers asked themselves if a prohibition was really necessary. It is simple arithmetic to conclude that the fewer the rules you must enforce, the fewer disciplinary actions you have to take. Equally important may be the dimunition of deviancies motivated by a sense of outrage at rules that are considered unfair and inconsequential.

MAKE THE LIST RELEVANT

Although not separate from the necessity of making a list minimal, there is the necessity for making your list of rules relevant. This requires that a teacher have a clear idea of the objectives of the particular course or homeroom class he is teaching. In terms of the considerations cited in the first part of this chapter, making a list relevant would consist of making sure that a majority of the classroom rules were firmly based on educational considerations. Chewing gum, the length of a boy's hair, the tightness of trouser hiplines, and the length of the girls' skirts—many of these might be taken off the deviancy list if a major criterion were educational relevancy.

MAKE THE LIST MEANINGFUL

In later chapters we shall refer to the beneficial effects of control techniques that are task-oriented rather than approval-oriented. If a teacher has made a list of rules that are both minimal and relevant, it should be a short easy step to make that list meaningful to his students. Rules which bear a logical relationship to the educational tasks at hand are difficult for students to write off as dictatorial caprice. Miss Neff insisted that the students in her English class fold their papers lengthwise and place their names on the outside of the folded work. She refused to accept a paper until it was done according to proper form, but her students seldom complained. At the beginning of each semester of English, Miss Neff took great pains to explain to the class that her system made it easy to avoid grading a student on the way she felt toward him instead of the content and mechanics of his writing.

She pointed out that if the names were put on the outside of the back of the paper, she could then unfold them all, read and grade them without looking at the name. She explained that this should result in a fairer grade for everyone.

MAKE THE LIST POSITIVE

In a later chapter, we will point out that a student learns proper classroom behavior by doing it and feeling rewarded for his efforts. Although a rule may always imply its opposite, a positive statement offers a goal to work toward rather than a veiled threat to avoid.

Mr. Martin found that his elementary science students could learn a lot from one another if they conversed about the experiments they were doing at their tables. At the same time, the noise volume had sometimes risen too high for effective work. He solved this problem neatly by describing a just-above-a-whisper "science voice" which he asked his students to put on as soon as they came through the door. To insist that pupils use their "science voice" is a much more attractive way to state the rule than to declare, "There will be no loud talking in this room!"

Summary

The classroom teacher defines behavior and misbehavior by the kinds of rules he makes and enforces in his room. Although each teacher makes a somewhat different list, most of them are based on moral, personal, legal, safety, and educational considerations.

If the number of disciplinary actions a teacher takes is to be diminished, a minimal list of rules is a prerequisite. The list may be made minimal by insisting that each item be relevant to the objectives of the course and meaningful to the students. Stating the list in a positive manner will make it a more effective set of guidelines than if it were stated as a series of prohibitions.

References

Crispin, D. *Discipline Behaviors of Different Teachers.* Unpublished paper read at AERA, Chicago, 1966.

Greene, J. E. Alleged misbehaviors among senior high school students. *Journal of Social Psychology,* 1962, *58,* 371–382.

James, H. W. Punishments recommended for school offenses. *Elementary School Journal,* 1928, *29,* 129–131.

Pressey, S. L., *et al. Life: A Psychological Survey.* New York. Harper and Brothers, 1939.

Schrupp, M. H. and C. M. Gjerde, Teacher growth in attitudes toward behavior problems of children. *Journal of Educational Psychology,* 1953, *44,* 203–214.

3

The Deviants: Why Students Make Trouble

Larruping larry—a small blonde tiger with flailing fists—was at it again. Battle 1 had occurred on the way to school that morning, and the safeties had not considered it serious enough to report to the principal. Battle 2 had taken place in gym class during the second school hour and got Larry an "F" in deportment for the day. Now here he was again in the "drink of water and lavatory line" pummeling the boy in front of him as though his life depended upon it.

Mr. Grange hauled him out of line and held him firmly until the flailing ceased. He was glad to be dealing with the little soft fists of a six-year-old and tried to imagine, momentarily, what he would do if Larry were fifteen. Dismissing the thought with the rueful recognition that he was woefully out of shape, Jack Grange led the subdued Larry back to the science room and began to go through the ancient, stereotyped ritual of scolding, threatening, and punishing that seems to rise up unbidden from the deep wells of a teacher's subconscious.

But Jack's mind withdrew for a moment, allowing the rest of his organism to continue the time-honored routine. "What's gotten into this formidable little tyke?" He mused, "What makes him so hard to handle? What sets him off like that? What kind of an approach might really get to the core of the trouble?"

As Mr. Grange's mind and body fused once more, he found himself sending Larry off to homeroom with the final "no more fights today" cliché! As the explosive little chap trudged off down the hall, Mr. Jack Grange, elementary science teacher, knew that he had failed the child once again. But there was the sixth grade already restless in their seats waiting to be enlightened about the probable atmospheric conditions of Saturn and Jupiter.

What Makes Children Misbehave?

Mr. Grange's question about what had "gotten into" Larry is a carry-over from the ancient times when the "demon theory" was accepted. At that time the answer to all such questions lay in the type of evil spirit that had entered the child's body. Another current phrase "I don't know what possessed him" arises from the same mystical approach. About the only thing to recommend such a theory is its implication that something outside the deviant is influencing his actions. There is no doubt that his self-control is limited by his past experience.

IGNORANCE

Ignorance of the rules is certainly one of the reasons for a child becoming a deviant. This is especially true during his first encounter with a teacher. Even if a student is presented with a neatly organized set of bylaws, he never really knows which statutes are operational and which are just on paper. As every seasoned substitute teacher knows, classes have a very practical way of solving this problem. They simply proceed to try the teacher out to see what they can "get away with."

Lest you think that the "trying out" procedure is a proof of the innate perversity of students, it should be pointed out that being in a situaiton where they really don't know the ground rules can be very anxiety-producing. It is analogous to diving into a gravel-pit swimming hole without being sure where the sharp rocks and bales of barbed wire are situated. Kounin and Gump (1961) found that even kindergarten children were able to differentiate between the verbal and actual rules of the classroom at the end of their first week in school.

CONFLICTING RULES

Conflicting social rulebooks is another situation in which students become deviants. William C. Kvareceus (1945) has continued to point out that many delinquents have learned the lessons of their neighborhoods too well. When the behaviors that brought results at home are deemed improper or immoral at school, a student becomes the victim of negative transfer of training.

Teachers born and trained in a middle class "cloister" are apt to be traumatized by the language and appearance of children who come from the center-of-the-city homes. Many a show-and-tell period has been discontinued, because the teacher could not bear either the subjects that were told about nor the language used in the telling.

The lad who has learned that the way to gain status in his neighborhood is to knock down every kid that taunts him is in for a great surprise when he tries to operate this way in most public schools. Kagan (1958) points out that many child behaviors are just imitations of some adult model. If that model behaves in ways that are not acceptable to the teacher in a given situation, the hapless mimic is in for trouble indeed.

It is obvious that a number of students may become deviants, merely because they have failed to discriminate between the rules of the home and school situations.

FRUSTRATION

Reactions to thwarting often take the form of deviancies in the classroom. Redl and Wattenberg (1960) imply this when they categorize a number of influence techniques as "task-assistance." John Dollard (1939) and others have presented quite an array of evidence supporting a frustration-aggression hypothesis. More recently Yarrow (1948) has demonstrated that aggression in children increases significantly after they have experienced failure.

There are at least three sources of frustration in a classroom that may impinge upon any student: the teacher, his classmates, and the activities. Any and all of these could push a student toward deviancy.

There were no doubt a number of students in Mr. Linker's algebra class (Chapter 1) who were frustrated by the detention period thrust upon them by Mr. Beggs, the principal. It would not have been surprising to see the number of deviants increase after such mass punishment. As the person in charge of the classroom, a teacher often finds himself thrust into the role of chief frustrator of his students.

A second source of thwarting may be the deviant's classmates. Lee Cronbach (1963) asserts that peer approval is a strong and basic need, often motivating student behavior. If a student is an isolate or reject in his own classroom, he might be expected to react with aggression to this intolerable situation.

Another researcher (Lorber, 1966) recently found that children who are socially unacceptable to their classmates tend to act in a disruptive, attention-seeking manner in the classroom. Although it may well be that their deviant behavior contributed to their loss of social acceptance, Lorber believes that these unfortunate actions are attempts by the socially ineffective child to temporarily appease his ego needs.

The difficulty of the subject matter itself may influence a student to become a deviant. One boy in a freshman algebra class was continually in trouble for not paying attention in class. Not only was he mentally absent when asked to recite, but he often failed to hear the most obvious assignments. When the truth of the matter was brought to light, daydreaming was his way of escaping from a situation where failure had become a daily experience. After the teacher helped him obtain a programmed text so that he could catch up with the other students, Sam was able to pay attention in class with much less effort. It is probable that many of the cases of inattention that prompted its addition to the list of deviancies in Chapter 2, were the direct result of such a frustrating situation.

DISPLACEMENT

Displaced feelings account for the misbehavior of some deviants. Just as inappropriate actions may be transferred into the classroom from an outside environment, so inappropriate feelings are often displaced upon the people and objects in the school. Bernadine was quite open about the fact that she could not stand Mr. Williams or his social studies class. She was always mumbling something nasty under her breath or bursting into tears at the slightest hint of disciplinary action. She assiduously any way.

Upon talking with the other teachers that taught Bernadine, avoided him in the hallway and refused to cooperate with him in Mr. Williams was aghast to find that his troublesome student seemed to be a model young lady in all the rooms except his. He took his problem to the assistant principal where the following story was revealed.

Bernadine and her mother lived in a cold-water flat together. The father had just left them for the third time that year. At least once a week over the past six months, the father had come home drunk and beaten his wife and daughter savagely. Both mother and daughter were convinced that men were beasts. Poor Mr. Williams was the only male teacher in the building and was the unwilling recipient of Bernadine's father-inspired hatred.

In a recent study of Thurston, Feldhusen and Benning (1964), several of the following factors appeared again and again in the home situations of children who were constant classroom deviants:

1. The discipline by the father is either lax, overly strict, or erratic.
2. The supervision by the mother is at best only fair, or it is downright inadequate.
3. The parents are either indifferent or even hostile toward the child.
4. The family members are scattered in diverse activities and operate only somewhat as a unit or perhaps not at all.
5. The parents find it difficult to talk things over regarding the child.
6. The husband-wife relationship lacks closeness and equality or partnership.
7. The parents find many things to disapprove of in their child.
8. The mothers are not happy with the communities in which they live.
9. The parents resort to angry physical punishment when the child does wrong. Temper control is a difficult problem for them at this time.
10. The parents believe they have little influence on the development of their child.
11. The parents believe that other children exert bad influences upon their child.

12. The parents' leisure time activities lack much of a constructive element.

13. The parents, particularly the father, report no church membership. Even if members, their attendance tends to be sporadic.

The transfer into the classroom of the parent-inspired hostilities of such children could certainly be at the base of their perennial deviancy.

Sam was always taking mean digs at the other students in Miss Smedly's class. He not only made fun of their recitations and art work, but he often poked them with his pencil or tripped them on the playground. In addition, Sam seemed to have an inordinate need for Miss Smedly's approval. It seemed as though he was always shouldering aside the others to gain the undivided limelight.

A brief talk with his mother revealed that Sam was a middle child in the family. He could not hope to compete successfully with the older brother who was both a brilliant student and a natural athlete. When he tried out the baby talk that seemed to work for his younger brother, his parents told him to grow up and stop acting like a two-year-old. It was apparent that Sam had transferred into the schoolroom his angry feelings toward his brothers and was taking them out on his undeserving classmates.

Often a student may be difficult to deal with, because he has a bad aftertaste from his experiences with another teacher or class. He may transfer his negative feelings for a cruel, sarcastic teacher to another who is really quite kind and considerate. A student, who has learned to hate social studies in another school, may misbehave in the social studies class in the new school simply because he has transferred those old feelings to a new situation. The unfortunate result is that he often causes the new teacher to feel the same way about him that the former one did, and the cycle begins all over again.

Although it is true that positive feelings are also transferred from old situations to new ones, they seldom pose any problems for the teacher. He usually assumes that students' good behavior is a direct and deserved result of his pedagogical expertise.

Summary

In this chapter, we have described some classroom deviants and some forces that probably contribute to their misbehavior. Ignorance, conflicting rulebooks, and social or academic frustration have been cited as factors predisposing a student to become deviant.

Displaced feelings about parents, siblings, former teachers, and former courses have all been listed as possible contributors to classroom misbehavior.

References

Cronbach, L. J. *Educational Psychology*, Second Edition. New York. Harcourt, Brace and World, 1963.

Dollard, J., N. E. Miller, L. W. Doob, O. H. Mowrer, and R. R. Sears. *Frustration and Aggression*. New Haven. Yale University Press, 1939.

Kagan, J. The concept of identification. *Psychological Review*, 1958, 65, 296–305.

Kvareceus, W. C. *Juvenile Delinquency and the School*. New York. World Book Company, 1945.

Lorber, N. M. Inadequate social acceptance and disruptive classroom behavior. *Journal of Educational Research*, 1966, 59, 360–362.

Redl, F. and W. Wattenberg. *Mental Hygiene in Teaching*, Second Edition. New York. Harcourt, Brace and World, 1960.

Thurston, J. E., J. F. Feldhusen, and J. J. Benning. *Classroom Behavior: Background Factors and Psycho-social Correlates*. Madison, Wisconsin. State Department of Public Welfare, 1964.

Yarrow, M. R. Problems of methods in parent-child research. *Child Development*, 1963, 34, 215–226.

4

The Teacher: One Cause
of Misbehavior

CAROL DENLER burst into agonizing tears. She was sure that she could never become a good accounting teacher and she was ready to quit school.

Mr. Joel, her college supervisor, was quite unprepared for this sudden and unexpected disaster. In his most professional manner, he tried to quiet the pretty young student teacher so that they could make some sense of the situation. Several Kleenex tissues later the following story blurted forth:

Miss Denler had been assigned to Mr. Thomas's business classes for twelve weeks of student teaching. Mr. Thomas, an expert critic teacher, had begun in the usual way by allowing Carol to observe his methods and get used to the class situation. Gradually he had worked her into the schedule until she was handling a full load of typing, shorthand, and accounting classes. Everything seemed to be going well when the one accounting class suddenly became unmanageable.

The girls in this class unaccountably turned on Miss Denler and seemed bent on sabotaging her every plan. They refused to hand in their papers on time. They made barely audible remarks about her appearance when she was trying to explain the work to the class. There were even several instances of out-and-out open defiance of the rules she was trying to enforce.

Because she was afraid that Mr. Thomas would give her a low grade in student teaching, she had kept these incidents a secret until the situation got so bad that she had fled to her college supervisor in a complete emotional dither.

Fifteen minutes after Miss Denler left, Mr. Joel was talking to the critic teacher on the phone. Mr. Thomas apologized for not looking in more often and promised to get to the bottom of the situation the next morning. He added that his student secretary was a member of the class and could help him fill in the details with more accuracy. At four the next afternoon, the critic teacher made the following revealing report to the college supervisor.

The boys in the accounting class had become quite infatuated with their pretty young teacher. They found out by trial and error that every time they asked for help with a posting problem, she would seat herself on the table near them, lean down close to them and make suggestions about how the problem should be approached. Reinforced by her close proximity, the boys deluged her with posting questions and vied with one another for her attentions.

According to Mr. Thomas's frank little secretary, Miss Denler was taking an unfair advantage of her position as a student teacher and had no business flirting with "their boys." The secretary added that Miss Denler wore her skirts too short and her blouses too tight for a teacher. She admitted openly that the girls hated the student teacher and were out to cut her academic throat.

When Mr. Joel explained the situation to Miss Denler, she was aghast. It was obvious from the look of disbelief on her face that she had been completely (and consciously) oblivious to what had been going on in the accounting class. She was so embarrassed that Mr. Joel was afraid she wouldn't go back to the class the next day.

Showing more pluck than he had expected, Miss Denler did return to her duties in the accounting class. For the rest of the time, she observed three rules carefully: she dressed in apparel that could not possibly be construed as provocative, answered the boys' questions in a business-like manner from a discrete distance, and never once sat on the tables again. She received an A in student teaching for that term.

Miss Denler's dilemma is a dramatic, but not unheard of, example of the fact that there are many situations in which teachers may unwittingly cause students in their own class to become deviant. In this chapter we will explore several of these situations so that our readers may understand and avoid them.

How Can Teachers Cause
Student Misbehavior?

In the last chapter we pointed out that ignorance of the rules and several varieties of classroom frustration could all be responsible for some of the deviant responses that students act out. It goes without saying that teachers who allow these situations to exist are in a sense causing students to misbehave. Although not entirely separate from these considerations, there are several other patterns of teacher behavior that can trigger student deviancies in uncomfortable amounts.

PLAYING THE ABSOLUTE DICTATOR

Both Redl (1942) and White (1960) describe the emotional reaction of student groups to the autocrat. The dictator has been called a tyrant, sadist, hard-boiled autocrat, and many other less complimentary names, but his intent seems always the same— to call all the shots. In one of those delightful flights of fantasy which caricature a person by carrying his behaviors to the absurd, one academic dictator's orders were re-enacted in the following way by one of his fifth-grade subjects. "Now you may open your books. Now you may read. Now you may put your name in the upper left-hand corner two centimeters from the edge. Now you may practice your spelling list. Now you may go to the lavatory. Now you may breathe!"

In a way the dictator establishes a sort of permanent atmosphere of frustration in the classroom, rewarding only the willing serf for his efforts. In light of our discussion in the last chapter, you will not be surprised to learn that most students respond to the dictator with a great deal of anger, but you may be unaware of some of the ways this anger is displayed.

If the tyrant is formidable enough, the anger may never be turned against him, at least not in his presence. Several studies have shown that students often wait until the leader is absent before they give vent to their aggression. Mrs. Stroud was a sturdy woman of sixty who ruled the fifth grade with an iron hand. Things always went well in her little kingdom and behavior problems were virtually unthinkable. Any unfortunate deviant who forgot his place for a moment was soon terrified into submission. [The glowering advance of this hulking woman was enough to make the bravest Jack in the class slide hurriedly back down his beanstalk to safety.]

But one morning the building custodian was witness to an awesome sight. Vandals had broken into the school sometime over the weekend and had virtually laid waste to Mrs. Stroud's room. Files were overturned, money was stolen, and ink was splashed on the walls and desks. Every window had been shattered from the inside, and papers were scattered about in complete disarray. One could almost visualize the anger that had been unleashed in that room the night before.

The janitor, hurrying into the adjacent social studies room, hardly dared predict what damage he might find there. To his surprise, neat piles of ballots were still in place awaiting the mock election to be held in class the next day. A sum of money collected for the Heart Fund was still safe in the unlocked top desk drawer. Nothing in that room had been touched by the weekend intruders.

As in all too many cases of this kind, the vandals were never caught, but those who understand the feelings that are stirred up by the dictator wouldn't be surprised to learn that Mrs. Stroud had been partly responsible for this destructive insurrection.

But formidable tyrants like Mrs. Stroud often cause other more serious deviancies of which they may not even be aware. In order to protect themselves, students serving under a teacher-dictator form their own "gestapo." As mass punishment is often used when the teacher is unable to find a culprit, each child protects himself by informing on the others. A regular secret service develops to the point where a would-be deviant is convinced that even the walls have ears.

[If the dictator becomes ill, an explosive situation may await an unsuspecting substitute teacher.] If she tries to use more democratic methods or is a bit less formidable as an autocrat, the students may literally run her out. Unfortunately, assistant principals often interpret this as a sign of incompetence on the part of the substitute and put her on their blacklist. Sadder still, the same administrators may laud the dictator as an exemplary teacher because she "can handle tough classes."

[Finally, the anger generated in the students of such an autocrat may be displaced upon one or more of the class weaklings after school. Frank Buck is supposed to have revealed the fact that he was never able to bring the weakest monkeys back alive.* After several healthy monkeys were captured and put in a cage for shipment, the weakest one or two were invariably dead on arrival at their destination.

Many a parent is at a loss to understand why the other children taunt or beat up one child night after night on the way home from school. When situations like this are investigated, it often develops that the child is one who can't or won't fight back. The frustration-triggered angers of the day can be safely displaced on those who will absorb the punishment. In those cases where a child seems to ask for trouble, a day with a tyrant will almost assure him of getting it.

Occasionally, some teacher tries to play the role of the dictator and fails. When the frustrations are great and the threat of punishment lacks conviction, a "fifth column" soon develops to sabotage the teacher. Unlike the case of the successful dictator, the students cohere against the teacher and victimize only those who like him (Redl, 1942).

Miss Toll was hired to teach English in a rural high school at the edge of a small village. Believing that a successful teacher must "start tough," she assumed the role of a dictator for a greater part of the first semester. Afraid that she would be unsuccessful, she was unnecessarily sarcastic and made petty and unrealistic demands upon her students. Several times boys in the class were moved to open defiance of her authority and found that she did not carry out her threats. Planned deviancies began to increase. Books were dropped on the floor at prearranged signals, chalk and erasers disappeared just before the teacher was going to use them, and weird noises constantly emanated from different locations in the room when the teacher's back was turned.

One day about the middle of the year the class saboteurs had drawn up a master deviancy plan. They obtained a supply of exploding toy caps and placed two in the steel supports of each desk seat in the English room. When the first-hour class came in and flopped resignedly in their seats, the sharp staccato of

* Frank Howard Buck (1884–1950) was an American jungle explorer who secured wild life without hurting them and sold them to U.S. zoos. He wrote *Bring 'Em Back Alive* in 1930.

thirty-five cap explosions bombarded the air. Taken completely unaware, Miss Toll fled the room in tears amid the nervous laughter of her class. She was unable to return to her post that semester and had to be replaced by substitutes for the remainder of the year.

The teacher who plays the role of absolute dictator may be a direct or indirect cause of many deviancies. If they do not occur in her presence, they may take place while she is gone or be displaced upon innocent third parties at other times.

BEING A MATINEE IDOL

The Miss Denler whose story opened this chapter was an example of an unwitting Matinee Idol. Redl (1942) would describe her as the "object of affectional drives." Other less psychoanalytic observers might just say that the boys had a crush on her. This phenomenon occurs most often at the high-school level, as this is the time that adolescents are making the transition from their parents as love objects to others nearer their own age. An intermediate stage in the process is often a more mature individual like a teacher who possesses both parental and peer-love-object qualities. The fresh-out-of-college teacher fits this category all too well.

In Miss Denler's case, deviancies arose because of the feelings engendered in the students of her own sex. They felt that their chances of making a hit with the boys were thwarted by Miss Denler's presence and actions and proceeded to direct their aggression at the person whom they perceived to be the cause of the frustrating situation. The fact that the student teacher allowed herself to be flattered by the boys 'attention made matters inestimably worse. It was only after she ceased her familiarity with the boys that she regained control of the class. Boys can become similarly irritated with a male Matinee Idol who flirts with the girls in their class.

Although not related closely to classroom deviancy as such, there are other knotty problems that can arise for the teacher who is unaware of his position as a Matinee Idol. Jim Friend always made his colleagues at Middleton High feel as though he cared a great deal about each of them. When Jim met them in the hall he never rushed by with the usual "Hello" or "How are you" that one expects. Invariably he would stop, put his hand on his fellow teacher's shoulder and talk briefly about something of mutual interest.

For this reason, teachers at Middleton were shocked to hear that Jim was being called before the school board on a morals charge. An inquiry into the situation brought to light the following story. One of the high-school girls developed a crush on Mr. Friend and began to stop him in the hall and on the street on one pretext or another. As was his custom, Jim Friend often talked to his female student with his hand on her shoulder. This habit, together with an active imagination on the part of the student, soon had started the story that Mr. Friend was taking indecent liberties with the girls at the high school. Several parents called the principal to protest the rehiring of such a teacher. One member of the school board demanded a special meeting to face Mr. Friend with the charges. Although Jim Friend was finally exonerated of all charges, it was a most uncomfortable year for him at Middleton High.

In order to illustrate that the Matinee Idol is probably always at least in part responsible for his own troubles, let it be said that those teachers who fail to respond to flirtations and who consistently show no favorites, soon discourage this brand of idolatry. There are some teachers on the other hand whose own needs prompt them to respond in ways that make the matter much worse.

Jill Star was a shapely little blonde who was hired to teach at Mill Center. Her collegiate record was quite excellent, and the principal felt fortunate to have obtained her to replace a teacher who was retiring. When the boys from senior English saw the new teacher walk into the room, several were moved to make low whistles of admiration and were overjoyed when she blushed obviously and became visibly flustered. Though she quickly regained her poise, it was apparent to all that the attention had gotten to her.

In the months that followed, the boys tried many strategies to gain her favor. For some unknown reason, Miss Star chose to discipline all deviants by making them sit in front of the class near her desk. Several boys took the bait and vied with each other for this position of honor, where they would gaze fondly at her. This action brought more blushes from Jill, and less English was taught with each succeeding day. Although a friendly principal tried to point out ways that disciplinary trouble could be avoided, the young teacher could not seem to extricate herself from the situation.

On the night of graduation, Miss Star went out on a date with a senior boy, confirming the principal's suspicion that there was more to the bad situation than a few obstreperous students. As the school board was outspoken on such matters, she was asked to resign immediately.

Although the Matinee Idol may not wish it so, he has become a love-object for one or more of his students. In- and out-of-school deviancies may result, if he does not take steps to prove that he is a mature adult who is interested in students as such and is not vulnerable to their attempts to gain his favor.

BECOMING A NONENTITY

Mr. Gale was convinced that one of the greatest ills of public school education was its suppression of the creative impulses of its students. Having read and applauded articles about "other-directed men who become sheep in gray flannel suits," he was determined that in his art class no such crime would be perpetrated. His approach was to lay out the materials necessary for work with several media and retreat to his own canvas, allowing each student to initiate an individual project and carry it out at his own speed. Mr. Gale made it quite clear to his students that their grade would not depend upon how many projects they turned out.

When a student came to him for help, he would either respond with, "What do you think?" or "Any way you want to do it is all right with me." If pressed for more direction, Benjamin Gale would invariably recite three or four approaches that the student might take and leave it to him to decide which he would use.

After a few weeks of this treatment, several different phenomena began to take shape. A revolving card game developed in the far corner among the boys who had taken art for a snap course. Little knots of giggling girls would assemble daily by the windows overlooking the athletic field. Several students brought textbooks from other subjects and used the period to catch up. Little scuffling bits of horseplay were on the increase, and the number of students who worked seriously at a project became fewer and fewer.

The climax to the story came on a Friday when three events brought Mr. Gale out of retirement. Dick Snead was one of the few students whom Mr. Gale considered to have real artistic promise. From the first day Dick had seemed eager to begin work and kept at it until he had arrived late several times at his next class. In his own mind Mr. Gale thought of Dick as a sort of human proof that his technique of teaching was effective. The week before, Mr. Gale had had to exert considerable self-control to keep from pointing out a perspective error that he knew would eventually ruin the effect of Dick's painting. But sounds of muffled fury emanated from behind Dick's canvas and Mr. Gale was horrified to see the muscular lad slash his hard work to ribbons and stamp unceremoniously out the door.

Visibly agitated by Dick's violent exit, the others began milling about nervously. Even the card game broke up. Two boys were soon pushing each other in prelude to a fight. Bits of clay began to fly about the room spattering here and there on the white walls. The volcano was preparing to erupt.

At this instant Mr. Volker, the principal, stepped into the room. Somehow avoiding the barrage of clay, he shouted the mob down, banished them all to study hall for the rest of the hour, and ordered them to show up after school to clean up the mess. For the next thirty minutes Mr. Gale and Mr. Volker planned some drastic reforms in the way art would be taught in the days to come.

A number of studies have described the effects of an impersonal, laissez-faire approach to leadership. (Thompson, 1944; White, 1953; Smith, 1960; Ryan, 1952.) The teacher who tries to be a *nonentity*, even for idealistic reasons, may be in for trouble. Without any structure, even art becomes filled with unpleasant feelings of pointlessness. For the earnest novice who sets his goals too high, a teacher who refuses to lend an expert hand in times of frustration may be a party to both deviancy and disillusionment.

Summary

Several inappropriate leadership styles have been described in this chapter. Each of them is likely to contribute to student misbehavior in class and outside of school.

The *absolute dictator* frustrates his classes so completely that they are driven to displace their hostility in destructive ways.

The *Matinee Idol* infuriates one half of the students in her classes by thoughtlessly flirting with the other half.

The *nonentity* contributes to the chaos in his own art class by refusing to give any guidance to his immature pupils.

These sketches show how a teacher may be a primary cause for his own disciplinary problems.

References

Redl, Fritz. Group emotion and leadership. *Psychiatry,* 1942, *4,* 513–596.

Ryans, David G. A study of criterian data. *Educational and Psychological Measurement,* 1952, *12,* 333–344.

Smith, L. M. *Pupil Expectations of Teacher Leadership Behavior,* 1960. Unpublished final report, U.S. Office of Education Cooperative Research Project 570 (8183).

Thompson, G. G. The social and emotional development of preschool children under two types of educational programs. *Psychological Monograph,* 1944, *56,* No. 5.

White, Ralph and R. Lippitt. Leader behavior and member reaction in three social climates. In Dorwin Cartwright and Alvin Zander (Eds.), *Group Dynamics.* Evanston. Row-Peterson, 1960, 527–533.

5

Control Techniques:
Antiseptic Influence

MR. POOLE was at his wits end again. It was just far enough along on Friday afternoon that he had begun to relax and let his mind go through its weekly T.G.I.F. routine. It had been one thing after another that week at Peerless Junior High. Broken windows had greeted them on Monday morning; the washrooms had been flooded on Wednesday; yesterday was the rescheduling nightmare that always went with the taking of class and individual pictures; and now this on Friday afternoon.

Mr. Slater, the custodian, came puffing in from servicing a girls' washroom between the fifth- and sixth-hour classes. Lowering his voice to a hoarse whisper so that the school secretary could not overhear, he described in lurid detail a message he had found written in Purple-Passion lipstick on the wall. The inscription was well laced with code-negative, four-letter words and Mr. Slater's grim expression belied the twinkle in his eyes as he went over the missive for the fifth time.

Mr. Poole was about to do his administrative duty and go down to view the evidence, but the energetic custodian assured him that he had scrubbed the message off immediately, so that no one else would have to look at such filth. It was at that moment that a plan occurred to the harried principal.

Throwing on the intercom switches, he broke into all the seventy-five sixth-hour classes with a "now hear this" that would have made any boatswain jealous. In one minute, every student and teacher in the building knew that someone had written an obscene note in the girls' restroom. They knew that Mr. Poole wanted the culprit to turn herself in before the end of the hour. They were also informed that no one would receive his class pictures the next week until the mystery was solved and the criminal apprehended.

As you can well imagine, not much learning took place at Peerless during the remainder of the afternoon. There was an undertone of nervous conversation in every class. Notes flitted silently back and forth across the rooms. Petitions of protest against mass punishment were already being worded in the minds of some of the young rebels, and requests for passes to the girls' washrooms increased 50 per cent above the normal number.

Between sixth and seventh hours, the girls' lavatories were so crowded that several girls were late to their last class. Although Mr. Poole had not said which washroom was the scene of the crime, every girl thought it might be the one on her floor. Every tile on every wall within reach was gone over with the thoroughness of the FBI for some trace of the intriguing message, but not so much as a smudge of Purple-Passion lipstick was unearthed. As the day ended, the culprit had not come forth; thus the drama would have to be continued the next week.

Three days of the next week went by, and the mystery still had not been solved. Pictures were to be handed out on Thursday, but daily reminders on the intercom assured the students that they would be withheld until June if necessary. Then somebody "finked."

A girl who had entered the lavatory just as the author of the obscenity was leaving told what she knew to the principal, and the diminutive blonde criminal was apprehended, Purple-Passion lipstick and all.

Boatswain Poole came back on the intercom and informed all seventy-five classes that the malefactor had been caught and that pictures would be passed out on schedule. After assuring the students that the girl would be expelled, he complimented them on the fine citizenship shown by the majority and said he was sorry that a few delinquents had to make it so hard on the rest of the school.

What Are Some Outcomes of Good Control?

In judging the advisability of using the kinds of techniques employed by Mr. Poole, we must set down some guidelines for evaluation. There are those who will read the incident and conclude immediately that it was a good move because it worked. What they mean is that the deviant was apprehended and punishment was meted out. But as we shall see, several other things "worked" also.

THE DEVIANCY MUST CEASE

It almost goes without saying that, in order to be effective, a control technique must put an end to the misbehavior. It was evident in the case of both the "dictator" and the "nonentity" that the longer deviancies are allowed to persist, the more disastrous the situation can become. The point to remember is that cessation is not the only desirable outcome of a control technique.

CONTAGION MUST BE INHIBITED

In an earlier chapter we noted that "giant volcanoes from little tremors grow." There is pitifully little consolation in the fact that you have stopped one minor deviancy only to discover that your methods have made deviants out of the remainder of the class. In Chapter 6 we will discuss this "negative ripple effect" in some detail.

HUMAN RELATIONS MUST BE MAINTAINED

Redl and Wattenberg (1959) suggest that before deciding how to handle a deviancy, one should consider a two-pronged question: How will it affect the deviant's relationship with his classmates and with the teacher himself?

It would hardly do to gain the control and lose the student. As peer relationships are so important in the psychological life of a student, and as problems in this area can most certainly inhibit the educational process, any control technique that appreciably decreases a deviant's status in the eyes of his classmates may trigger more problems than it solves.

Similarly, there are a lot of tomorrows to be considered that will include the teacher's continued relationship with the deviant. Long after everyone has forgotten just what happened, the teacher and the deviant must interact in such a way that optimum learning will take place. If a control technique is selected that is too harsh or unfair, a deviant may become so angry or afraid that a constructive relationship with the teacher may be virtually impossible from that time on.

A third consideration involves the reaction of the class audience to the way a teacher controls a deviant. Although this matter will be considered at length in Chapter 6, it must be said here that improper handling of a deviancy may result in a change of the class attitude that will not only predispose them to further deviancies, but may seriously inhibit the learning process for days to come. You will remember that the unsuccessful "dictator" was finally driven out for her unwise use of control techniques.

LEARNING BECOMES MORE EFFICIENT

Although certainly not separate from other considerations, a control technique should improve the chances that learning will take place. If deviancies are occurring in profusion, these multiple distractions cannot help but cut down educational efficiency (Gnagey, 1960). An equally unfortunate situation arises when the control technique a teacher uses disrupts the learning atmosphere to a greater extent than the deviancy. In such a case, it might have been better to let the deviancy go unattended than to deal an even more devastating blow to the progress of the academic program.

LEARNING BECOMES MORE DESIRABLE

Someone has said that the kindergarten or nursery-school teacher is the most important figure in public education, because she sets the stage for the next twelve years of schooling. Actually, every teacher adds to or detracts from her students' love of learning. The emotional responses that she helps her classes to associate with school and the learning process may be as important as the subject matter that she had taken so many pains to present.

Control techniques that continually elicit negative feelings from deviants, and their classmates do their part in building up a host of emotional barriers to further learning. You may remember that in Chapter 2, we cited "teacher aftertaste" as one cause of deviancy that may be transferred from one classroom to another.

How Can the Principles Be Applied?

If we use these principles as guidelines for evaluating Mr. Poole's disciplinary procedures in handling the "lipstick obscenity incident," his actions don't seem as appropriate as they might have at first.

1. The deviancy did cease. Of course it had already ceased when the culprit walked out the door, but it did not recur that year.

2. Contagion was inhibited if one means that nobody else was moved to write on the wall with a lipstick.

3. Human relations were *not* maintained. Aside from the anguish that the deviant and her parents may have gone through during her period of banishment, we can be glad that Mr. Poole was not a classroom teacher. He would then have had to face the daily outrage of students who were to have been punished for someone else's misbehavior. He might also have witnessed the ostracism heaped upon the hapless ex-convict as soon as the student grapevine found out who had been responsible for all the upset.

4. Learning became *less* efficient. Not only were all seventy-five sixth-hour classes sabotaged by Principal Poole's intercom ultimatum, but the disrupted feelings of those students inhibited learning for nearly a full week. His continued warnings over the loudspeaker were hardly neutralized by his final admission that most of the students were good citizens.

5. Although the fact that this control technique was carried out by a principal rather than a classroom teacher may have somewhat diluted the effect, learning *did not* gain any positive effect from this experience. Aside from the bitter feelings that the deviant was sure to have toward school, numerous students

in the seventy-five classrooms at Peerless chalked it up as just one more proof that school was "for the birds," strengthening their resolve to take advantage of the opportunity to quit when they reached sixteen. **1474045**

Although we can readily sympathize with Principal Poole and realize that his reaction to the lipstick note was largely the result of the multiple frustrations of an impossible week, he would probably have been better off ignoring the whole incident. One such note, quietly scrubbed off, could hardly jeopardize either the educational or moral excellence at Peerless Junior High. It almost certainly could not stir up as much consternation as the techniques employed by the harassed principal during those two weeks.

WHAT ARE SOME CONSTRUCTIVE TYPES OF CONTROL?

One author (Redl, 1957) has characterized constructive control techniques as "antiseptic." These actions get the job done without a lot of destructive effects. In other words, constructive control techniques conform to all the guidelines we have just set up. They can be grouped into several types according to the specific function they perform.

SOME TECHNIQUES REDUCE FRUSTRATION

You will remember that we pointed out in earlier chapters that deviancy may be a reaction to frustration. Though an obvious remedy for such situations is the removal of those frustrating situations, it is helpful to spell out some specific ways in which this must be done.

The use of *diagnostic pretests* is one way to eliminate some subject matter frustrations before they arise. With all our talk about individual differences and readiness and "beginning where the child is," there are a startling number of teachers who "just start teaching." A practice like this spells frustration almost by definition.

Often an old unit final examination can be used as a diagnostic pretest. Two or three items can be selected to measure skills or knowledge in each of the several portions of the unit to come. Analysis of these results will show not only the aspects of the unit that will need the most emphasis for the whole class, but they will point out specific weaknesses of each student. If the results show a lack of background in some crucial area, homework assignments or special remedial help can be started immediately to forestall greater frustration and failure further along.

Redl and Wattenberg (1959) insist that some "helping over hurdles" will become necessary at times even in the best diagnosed classes. They point out that if a student becomes unruly because of his inability to perform some part of the assignment, the teacher's point of attack should be to help with the problem rather than make an issue out of the misconduct.

Miss Blake came to Prim Elementary School to teach music. She had begun in the sixth grade to teach several of the popular songs from recent family movies and records. The classes were responding well and Miss Blake was congratulating herself on having made this move.

In order to help her classes read music better, she determined to have them practice singing numbers assigned to each note so that they could get the idea of chords and intervals. Playing a three-note chord on the piano, the students were instructed to sing 1-3-5-3-1, etc. but only a handful sang at all.

Interpreting their lack of response as impudence, Miss Blake gave them a severe lecture about listening to instructions. She reminded them that they had done this for two years and could certainly perform better than that. When a boy in the front row raised his hand, the teacher informed him that they were here to learn music and not to talk.

After several more disheartening attempts to sing the numbers, nervous giggles and talking began to increase in the back rows. Miss Blake went bravely on, raising her voice a bit to drown out the talkers. The gigglers in turn raised their volume, until the teacher could take it no longer. Singling out the two boys who had been talking the loudest, she sent them to the principal's office with a note stating that they had been terribly rude and unruly and that she didn't want them back in class until they had apologized.

Mercifully, the bell rang, and the sixth-graders filed out on tiptoes. Miss Blake retired to the teachers lounge in a state of angry frustration. Finding a sympathetic colleague already there, she poured out her tale of woe. She was red-faced when she heard the other teacher's response.

The music teacher who had just retired had been working with the children for two years on their sight-reading skills. Unfortunately she had always used the syllable system. If Miss Blake had asked them to sing do-me-sol-me-do to her chord, she might have been pleasantly surprised.

In this case, a little diagnosis would have gone a long way toward making her first few weeks more pleasant. If she had recognized the hand in the front row as a plea for "hurdle help," much of the misbehavior might have been averted.

When one television program becomes uninteresting, even a first-grader knows enough to *change the channel*. But all too often the teacher ignores the signs of boredom that indicate the lesson he has planned is not going well. It is as though a change in the structure of the plan would be an admission of failure and that it is some index of valor to plod through the remainder of the lesson no matter what.

Mr. Barnes had been droning on for some time about the Frasch process for mining sulphur. He had covered the economic values of the product, the machinery used, and the properties of this nonmetal that made the process possible. He was suddenly aware that the class was not with him. Some were looking out of the window, some were passing notes, some were talking together covertly, and others were openly dozing. Realizing that it was time to "change the channel" through which the learning was supposed to be taking place, Mr. Barnes abruptly stopped his lecture and announced, "As you know, you are going to have to pass a test on this unit in a few days. One of the best ways to study for a test is to pretend that you are going to make out the exam and go through the text making up your own questions. In the next ten minutes, I would like each of you to go through the text description of the Frasch process and make up at least three questions that you would ask if you were making out the exam. When you finish, we will see if you can stump the rest of us."

Chemistry 1 suddenly came to life. Pencils were picked up. Books were opened. Notebooks became functional. Talking and note passing deviancies ceased abruptly. Not only was there optimum participation for the rest of the period, but on the end-of-the-week quiz, it was obvious that most of the students understood the Frasch process. Redl and Wattenberg (1959) would call this "restructuring the situation."

Temptation removal is another technique that may forestall classroom deviancies. Redl and Wineman (1957) noted that their ego-damaged boys at Pioneer House were easy prey to "gadgetorial seduction." Although the self-control of average children may be somewhat stronger, keeping tempting objects at a minimum will reduce a lot of the conflict-frustration basic to deviancy.

Lunch money that is locked up doesn't get stolen as often as money left unattended. Displays of artifacts that are placed some distance from desks aren't as likely to be a distraction or to disappear or be broken. Checking playthings at the teacher's desk until after school may avert many distracting deviancies during the day.

Routines may sound like deviancy producers, instead of control techniques. We often think of rules and regulations as additions to frustration, instead of methods for reducing it. But a whole host of frustrations may arise just because a student has some pressing need that he cannot communicate to the teacher or that he cannot take care of himself. Routines are merely approved ways of satisfying needs that commonly arise in the classroom.

Raising one's hand to signify the wish to speak is a way of averting the frustrations of either remaining silent or shouting others down. Having a lavatory pass is a way of facilitating a child's need to go to the bathroom when he could not even politely break into the teacher's interactions with other children. Passing paper, sharpening pencils, collecting notebooks can all be organized into routines that produce minimal frustration. Cellar (1951) found that teachers who had a well-worked-out set of routines had significantly fewer disciplinary problems.

When the demands of a situation are too much for a student for the moment, he should have some approved method of *strategic retreat*. Abbie was humiliated. She and Liz had begun laughing in the hall between classes, and now she couldn't stop. Everything seemed funny, and just when she thought she had regained control, Liz would catch her eye and it would begin all over again. People were beginning to look at her now, and the teacher was beginning to get annoyed. Abbie tried all the tricks she knew to mask her glee. She bit her lip, she pretended to be blowing her nose when she had to snicker; she told herself sternly not to be such a "jerk." But nothing helped. In the middle of an uncontrollable giggle, she suddenly realized that she had better get to the lavatory quickly or it would be too late. Abbie was embarrassed to death.

Somewhere outside the prison of her agonizing mirth, she heard Miss Good's welcome prescription, "Abbie, we won't get any social studies learned until you get over your giggles. Why don't you go over to the girls' lounge and pull yourself together. Come back whenever you are ready."

Redl and Wattenberg (1959) point out that it is important that this be a "nonpunitive exile" with the emphasis on "getting over it" rather than implied incarceration "until you can behave."

A *practice alert* can often forestall deviancies when the actual situation is encountered. The well-practiced fire drills are a fine example of this control technique. When all the moves are planned ahead so that each class knows the routine, situations seldom develop into panic even when the alert is a real one.

Mr. Olson was about to teach a unit on the various kinds of seeds and their function. The year before, his third-graders had participated in a near-catastrophe. A nature study guide had suggested that the prickly seeds of the burdock could be fashioned into interesting little baskets. Mr. Olson had determined that this was a good time to combine the aesthetic with the scientific and had asked all the children in the class to collect the burrs and bring them to school for the basket project.

After explaining the scientific aspects of "hitch-hiking" seed pods, he demonstrated the construction of the burr baskets and urged the children to make their own. Things went beautifully for awhile, and Mr. Olson was wondering why he hadn't done this every year. Then disaster struck!

Two or three children began to complain that their arms felt itchy. In about two minutes, half of the third-grade science class was scratching. Red welts began to rise on twenty-five little bare arms, and pandemonium began to build. Two little girls had burst into tears and were sent to the assistant principal for help. By the time the assistant principal got to the science room, Mr.

Olson had dumped all the burrs into the waste basket and was helping a chafing line of students wash off their arms in soap and water.

With the help of some soothing ointment that only assistant principals can produce at a time like this, the two adults managed to get things under control, and by the time the bell rang, most of the class was ready for gym.

Needless to say, this year Mr. Olson is not only excluding burdock baskets from his activities, but he carefully warns his students not to bring large samples of these hitch-hikers to school with their seed collections.

Comic relief often saves the day when other control techniques would have only made matters worse. Movie producers usually break up prolonged suspenseful situations with the antics of some "clown." A good laugh reduces the tension enough for the audience so that as the story approaches its climax, the suspense doesn't become too uncomfortable.

Mr. Vlasic was trying to prepare his debate squad for the county tournament. In order to motivate his affirmative team to sharpen up their case, he had just delivered the rebuttal for the negative team and completely devastated the presentation of the opposition. Furious at having been made a fool of, one of the boys on the affirmative team began to shout his outrage at the coach. Completely forgetting himself in the heat of his resentment, the irate lad referred to his teacher as a "stupid old man."

There was a dead silence as the whole team held their breath. Even the young attacker was shocked by what he had said. After a second or two of contemplation, Mr. Vlasic smiled, "Well now that we've got me classified, let's get on with the practice."

A gale of relieved laughter followed and the debate proceeded. Afterward a grateful young debater apologized appreciatively to an understanding coach.

The beneficial effects of *catharsis* are well known in clinical circles and can be nicely applied to the classroom. Whenever it is evident that a great deal of hostility has been built up by the multiple frustrations of a school program, a teacher can arrange for what Wattenberg and Redl (1959) call "irritability drain-off." Games such as "bombardment" or "dodgeball" perform this function admirably since a great deal of hostility can be released in a way that is neither antisocial nor dangerous. Teachers without benefit of gym equipment might hold gripe sessions in which irate students are encouraged to air their grievances. This latter method takes careful handling, however, since real catharsis often goes beyond the bounds of acceptable discussion of issues and too easily becomes focused on personalities.

Diagnostic pretests, hurdle-help, changing the channel, temptation removal, routines, comic relief and *catharsis* are all constructive control techniques that avoid, reduce, or remove deviancy-causing frustrations from the classroom.

SOME TECHNIQUES ACTIVATE STUDENT MOTIVES

Although there are times and places when any teacher might scoff at this assertion, most children want to be "good" most of the time. If this were not so, "blackboard jungles" would have overgrown the public schools long ago and the great American dream of free education for all would have disappeared in the tangle. Not only have students learned to behave, but they have learned a healthy respect for the fact that education in these times is the *sine qua non* for the good life. The following control techniques are based on these facts and are aimed at activating the positive motivation already present within most students.

As we suggested earlier concerning Mr. Poole's handling of the lipstick incident, ignoring a momentary breach of conduct may often be the most constructive "control technique" a teacher can employ. Several considerations that might indicate ignoring as the best policy are:

1. The misconduct may not be serious or dangerous.
2. The deviant may be generally well-behaved.
3. Calling attention to the event might destroy the learning atmosphere.
4. The deviant will probably not be "rewarded" by classmates for his misdeed.

Miss Tasher was holding a very successful discussion of the reign of Ghengis Khan in ancient Cathay. The class had read a portion of Marshall's *Caravan to Xanadu* (1953) and were eagerly comparing this account of Marco Polo's book adventures with that of the history text. Out of the corner of her eye, the history teacher noticed that Nancy Kim was busily manicuring and polishing her nails in the back row. As this practice had been specifically outlawed in the high school, a decision had to be made.

Miss Tasher quickly decided to ignore the incident this time, and the class went on without interruption until the ringing of the bell snatched the students back from Cathay to the more mundane routines of the school schedule.

Visual prompting is also effective in reactivating a student's wish to behave properly. In cases where ignoring a deviancy seems inappropriate or inadvisable, a teacher may still handle a deviancy with signals that help him get the deviant back to the business at hand without gathering an audience.

Miss Corda taught history at Junction High School. As is often the case, her assignment included two hours each day in which she was in charge of a study hall. Whereas many of the other study-hall teachers would use this time to correct papers or read at the front desk, Miss Corda wandered slowly from place to place surveying the situation from many angles. Whenever two students began a conversation, the teacher moved into a position where she could catch their eye. Usually a shake of her head or a motion with her hands was enough to break up the potential study hazard. Students who were already preparing their lessons were usually completely oblivious of the incident.

Motivational recharging may be necessary when interest in a project seems to be waning and boredom begins to override self-control. This is a time when the teacher can look over the progress a student has made and re-emphasize the importance of the venture.

Miss Jackson had assigned to Jill and Marsha the job of stuffing play announcements into envelopes and addressing them to the parents of the drama class. In the meantime the cast was rehearsing some of the more difficult parts of the second act. After preparing about ten envelopes, the two girls were beginning to interfere with the rehearsal. They giggled inappropriately when close girl friends acted out tense moments, in an effort to make them forget their lines.

At the end of one of the scenes, the teacher gave instructions to the cast about setting-up for the next act. She strode back to Jill and Marsha and made the following observation, "You girls will certainly have to hurry if you are going to finish the rest of these before five. Remember, if they aren't addressed and in the mail by five, they won't get to your parents in time for them to come to the play." The girls returned to their task with renewed vigor, and the rehearsal of the next act went off without an incident.

Redl and Wattenberg (1959) suggest that *defining the limits* may enable students who are already motivated to be "good" to avoid stumbling over a rule that they did not know existed. You will remember that in Chapter 3 we pointed out that "trying out the teacher" was one way students have of finding out what the rules of the game actually are.

Even for a group of students that is motivated to learn without unnecessary deviancy, it is often advisable to help them *make connections* between their behavior and its causes or consequences. Not only does this amplify the feedback that is so necessary for them to judge the appropriateness of their actions, but it can go a long way toward helping students understand their own behavior and that of their peers.

Mr. Nagy was having a hard time keeping several members of his swimming class from running on the wet cement around the pool. One day after he had had to speak sharply to several students, he called a number of the deviants over to a patch of concrete that had just been hosed off. He explained how much more slippery it was than the dry sidewalk outside the school. He then related a true story about a student who had suffered a brain concussion several years before as a result of a serious fall near the pool. At the end of the story, Mr. Nagy emphasized the "walk rule" again and explained why he had to be very strict in enforcing it. From that time on, running on the deck decreased greatly.

A *post mortem* session is often useful after a deviancy has been committed. It gives the teacher a chance to help a student see the causes for his misbehavior and avoid them in the future. Care must be taken to prevent this technique from turning into an "I told you so" session aimed at vindicating the teacher's unerring judgment.

Jerry Short was crying and holding his knee. Blood was oozing out of a nasty floor burn, and the child was in obvious pain. Miss Parsons' fourth-graders had just lined up for their lavatory break and a mad rush toward the door had resulted in Jerry's being shoved down on one knee. An old hand at such mishaps, Miss Parsons sent a friend to help Jerry get to the school nurse. She then calmly helped the class proceed through their lavatory time. After the class returned and Jerry came back from the nurse, the teacher helped her students talk the incident over. They all agreed that they didn't want others to get hurt, and that something had to be done to improve the lining-up procedure. After a little discussion, it was decided that if one row at a time lined up, there would be less chance of mishaps. The group also reaffirmed their intent to walk into line, because running could cause a bad accident.

Ignoring, visual prompting, recharging, defining limits, making connections and *post mortem sessions* are all techniques that are based on the assumption that most students are motivated to learn in a nondeviant manner most of the time. Their function is to activate constructive motives already learned by the students. They cannot be expected to be effective in situations where students have learned to be antiteacher, antischool or antilearning.

SOME TECHNIQUES IMPOSE EXTERNAL CONTROLS

Although the previous section dealt with methods of behavior control, it was limited to making use of controls already internalized by most students. As there are always some pupils who cannot or will not behave themselves in school, external controls must be used to reduce disruptive misbehavior. With this group of procedures more than any other, it is difficult to follow the guidelines set up at the beginning of this chapter so that control will remain antiseptic.

Protective restraint is sometimes necessary when a student loses his temper and aggresses against other students. In Chapter 3 when Mr. Grange held Larruping Larry until he calmed down, the external controls were forceful, but still antiseptic. Larry was being protected from hurting himself, and his classmates were being protected from Larry. It was only when the teacher began to scold and threaten that he departed from his antiseptic role. As we indicated there, this control is possible only when the teacher is much larger and stronger than the student. It differs radically also from the high-school teacher who is called upon to defend himself against the fists or weapons of one of his students.

Punishment is perhaps the most controversial of the control techniques that have been used in the public school. Positions vary from those who recommend that it never be used to those who believe that it should be used first and then all other techniques would not be needed.

In an earlier publication (Gnagey, 1965) we have pointed out that there is a great difference between retributive and restitutive punishment. If a student is asked to stay after school to make up work that he missed when he skipped class, this is more properly called *restitution* (Smith and Hudgins, 1964), as he is making right something which came about because he broke a rule. Restitution would also be the proper term for a case in which a culprit is made to pay for a window which he broke. Certainly it would not be pleasant to get along on a reduced allowance, but it still fits the "making it right" model. It would be correct also to apply the term restitution to an incident in which a student has used profanity or obscenity in the classroom and is asked to rephrase his comment in more acceptable words.

Retribution, on the other hand, involves getting back at a pupil who has upset the teacher's plans and has made him angry. It is based on a sort of "eye for an eye" philosophy that invokes the crude justice of hurting someone in order to even the score. Although it would be folly to say that teachers should never feel like getting even with a student, retributive punishment is most difficult to make antiseptic. If a teacher judges that a misdemeanor calls for punishment, he should take the following facts into consideration before using it:

1. Punishment will not erase the tendency to perform a deviant habit. The effect of painful consequences is to suppress the misbehavior for a time until the punisher is not present. Mrs. Stroud in Chapter 4 illustrated the principle that control by fear of punishment may cause students to take out their aggression in indirect ways that may be worse than the original misdeed.

2. Punishment does not teach the correct behavior. Unless there is a simple right way–wrong way choice, punishing a misbehavior fails to point out, explain, or demonstrate a behavior that would be acceptable in a similar situation. Restitution does a much better job of teaching an acceptable behavior in place of an unacceptable one.

3. Punishment often causes a student to avoid a situation rather than to improve it. Miller (1948) has shown how strong a motivator fear can be and how difficult it is to retrain an organism which has learned an avoidance response. If fear feelings are associated with teachers, subjects, or school in general, students will quickly learn ways to avoid all three. It is probable that a large number of school drop-outs are acting out of fear and disgust of the school situation and wish to avoid any more education at all costs.

4. Fear decreases the ability to solve problems creatively. A class that is controlled principally by fear of punishment will most likely become a rubber stamp for the teacher's way of doing things and will be unable to see other alternatives at all. The widespread use of fear-evoking punishment in our classrooms may actually discourage the production of the critical, innovative citizens that a democracy requires.

Protective restraint, restitution, and *retribution* are all control techniques that make use of external forces to keep order in situations where students cannot be motivated to use their own self-control.

Summary

In this chapter we have laid down several guidelines for the use of constructive control techniques. Borrowing heavily from the work of Redl and Wattenberg (1959), we listed and illustrated a number of teacher actions that have been successfully used to control classroom misbehavior. Some of these served to avoid or reduce frustrating conditions for the student. Another series of techniques was described in which the function was the activation of constructive motives within the pupil. In a fourth category several methods of imposing external controls were described and evaluated.

One of the principal goals of this chapter has been to increase the repertory of control techniques available to the reader so that he may be more able to choose an appropriate assortment for his particular needs.

References

Cellar, S. Practices associated with effective discipline. *Journal of Experimental Education*, 1951, *19*, 333–358.

Gnagey, W. J. Effects on classmates of a deviant student's power and response to a teacher-exerted control technique. *Journal of Educational Psychology*, 1960, *51*, 1–9.

Gnagey, W. J. *Controlling Classroom Misbehavior*. Washington, D.C., National Education Association, 1965.

Marshall, E. *Caravan to Xanadu*. New York. Farrar, Straus and Young, 1953.

Miller, N. E. Studies of fear as an acquirable drive: I. Fear as a motivation and fear reduction as reinforcement in the learning of new responses. *Journal of Experimental Psychology*, 1948, *38* 89–101.

Redl, F., and W. Wattenberg. *Mental Hygiene in Teaching*, Second Edition. New York. Harcourt, Brace and World, 1959, Chapter 13, Influence techniques.

Redl, F., and D. Wineman. *The Aggressive Child*. Glencoe, Illinois. Free Press, 1957.

Smith, L., and B. Hudgins. *Educational Psychology: An Application of Social and Behavioral Theory*. New York. Alfred A. Knopf, 1964, Chapter 9, Classroom discipline.

6

The Audience: Students
Influenced by Ripple

Miss robe announced: "I'm very interested in finding
out some things about films that we show in school." "I have
brought one with me today. I want you to watch it quietly,
without talking, so that you can rate it accurately when it is over."

Having made this little speech, Miss Robe turned out the
light and began showing a 10-minute film about living cells. At a
prearranged place in the film, the teacher pretended to scratch
her head. Immediately a boy, secretly trained beforehand, asked
in a loud voice, "Hey, is this thing about over?"

At this interruption Miss Robe shut off the projector and
addressed the deviant angrily, "Hey you! I told you not to talk.
You leave the room and report to the principal's office."

At this the deviant stood up and said in a very contrite
manner, "Yes ma'am, I'm sorry ma'am." He then strode to the
door and disappeared quietly into the hall.

As the door closed, the teacher turned on the projector again
and showed the remainder of the film, a sort of review of the
previous parts of the presentation. When the film was over, she
shut off the projector, turned on the lights, and left the room
quietly.

This was the scenario of one of a series (Gnagey, 1960) of
studies carried out under the direction of Jacob S. Kounin at
Wayne State University to ascertain what effects the disciplining
of one student had on those classmates who are audience to, but
not targets of the control technique. This chapter will describe

48

and illustrate these research findings as they apply to the improvement of discipline in the classroom.

WHAT INFLUENCES THE RIPPLE EFFECT?

Every lad who has ever enjoyed the excitement of hook-and-line fishing in a quiet pool can describe one kind of ripple effect in glowing detail. How often has he held his breath and strained his eyes for some slight movement of the float that might signal the presence of an unwary fish below. He will describe how more than once, when his attention has strayed to other parts of the pond, the concentric circles of wavelets from his bobbing cork have snatched his attention back to the business at hand and saved him the ignominy of going home with an empty stringer.

Kounin and Gump (1958) have taken the analogy of the bobbing cork and the ever-widening wavelets to represent the situation in a classroom when a teacher finds it necessary to discipline an erring student. Although the focus is on the interaction between the teacher and the deviant, unseen wavelets of influences are circling out and impinging upon the other members of the class who are witness to the altercation. This is called the *ripple* effect.

CLARITY

A *clear control* technique is one that specifies the deviant, the deviancy, and the preferred alternative behavior. The teacher who hears a disturbance in the rear of the room and yells, "Hey, you guys, knock it off back there," has articulated a control technique with almost no clarity at all. In addition to interrupting every other student within earshot, not even the deviants are sure that the reprimand was meant for them.

The same teacher might have moved back toward the noisy group and said, "Bill, Jack, and Paul, stop talking and get those algebra problems finished!" The clarity of this command is very high and can be expected to have two beneficial effects on the audience students:

1. They will be less likely to become deviant themselves.
2. Their learning behavior is less likely to become disrupted

than would be true for an unclear technique like the first one.

FIRMNESS

A *firm control* technique has an "I mean business" quality about it. This may be accomplished by the teacher's tone of voice, facial expression, or gestures. It may also be accomplished by what the Kounin group called "follow-through." *Follow-through* consists of some way of seeing to it that your disciplinary prescription is carried out.

Paul was playing a game of box hockey on the top of his desk using a pencil and a wad of notebook paper. His actions had commandeered the attention of most of the boys in his immediate vicinity, and Miss Blair's attempts to explain the intricacies of the inner ear were going unnoticed. She stopped abruptly and commanded in a stern voice, "Paul, put that paper in the waste basket and pay attention!"

Focusing her whole attention upon the benched hockey player, the teacher followed his progress to and from the waste-paper basket and only after he was properly seated again did she resume her efforts with the structure of the ear.

Firm control techniques have two advantages over bland ones: they not only increase the conformance of the deviant, but increase the cooperation of all witnesses who were focused upon the deviancy at the time it was occurring.

Researchers found that by the end of the first week in kindergarten, children were already responding only to the rules that were actually enforced (followed-through) and ignoring the verbal commands that didn't really carry any weight (Kounin and Gump, 1958).

ROUGHNESS

Mr. Bold taught elementary school music at Milford. It was his first experience at teaching below the high-school level, and he was finding it difficult to keep order. For a time he hit upon the following procedure for handling unwanted conversations in the music room: he would sneak quietly up behind them and shout angrily for silence. These unexpected blasts startled everyone in the room and the majority of the class were unable to concentrate on music for the remainder of the period. Mr. Bold soon realized that he was doing more harm than good with this approach.

Ten years later the Kounin group empirically supported Mr. Bold's conclusion (Kounin, Gump, and Ryan, 1961). In experiments at two levels in the elementary school, these researchers came to several conclusions. Even though the students who witness a teacher's use of threatening control techniques tended to rate him as a stronger disciplinarian and to consider the deviancies involved to be more serious, several negative effects were produced:

1. They produced a great deal of disruptive behavior among students who are witness to the control technique, even though they were not deviant themselves.
2. They did not keep witnesses from becoming deviant at a later time.
3. They caused witnesses to lower their estimation of the teacher's helpfulness, likeability, and fairness.

It became apparent that roughness was not just an increased degree of firmness, but in fact had opposite ripple effects upon the audience.

FOCUS

As a member of the Wayne State research team, Elizabeth Alden (1959) compared the ripple effects of *approval-focused* and *task-focused* control techniques. An approval-focused technique depends for its effect upon the relationship between the teacher and the deviant while a task-focused technique "makes connections" (Chapter 5) between the teacher's demand and the work to be accomplished.

In our opening scenario, when a boy talked out loud during a film showing, Miss Robe might have said, "I'm very disappointed that you talked when I asked you not to. I thought you had more respect for me than that." This would have been an approval-focused technique.

If she had chosen to use a task-focused technique, the film teacher might have declared, "You must be quiet during the film or else you will not be able to rate it afterward. We don't have time to see it a second time."

Working with fifth-graders, Miss Alden drew the following conclusions from her study:

1. Witnesses to task-focused techniques raised their estimates of the teacher's skill more than did witnesses to approval-focused techniques.
2. Interest in the subject matter increased in classes who witness task-focused techniques. Such was not the case for classes controlled by approval-focused techniques.
3. Audiences who believed their teacher to be an expert in his subject matter field reacted to his use of task-focused techniques by raising their estimates of his affection for them.
4. This combination of perceived expertness and the use of task-focused techniques influenced students to learn more from the lessons and feel less inclined to misbehave.
5. If the audience perceived a teacher as expert and affectionate toward children, his use of task-focused control techniques caused them to feel more inclined to discuss personal matters with him.

Without exception, these results indicated that task-focused control techniques have a more desirable ripple effect than do approval-focused methods.

THE DEVIANT'S RESPONSE

There were only two groups in which the deviant was trained to respond to Miss Robe's control technique as described in the opening scene of this chapter. Although the culprits were very submissive and apologetic in these experimental groups, they were trained to be defiant in two others.

In the two deviant groups, when Miss Robe said, "Hey you! I told you not to talk. You leave the room and report to the principal's office!," the deviants responded belligerently, "I'll leave the room, but I won't go to the principal's office. The heck with you." They topped off their performance by slamming the door as they left.

When the ripple effects of defiant responses were compared

with those of submissive ones, several significant differences appeared.

1. Witnesses to submissive deviants rated the teacher as "more capable of handling kids" than did the witnesses to defiant deviants.
2. The film teacher was rated as more of an expert on films in groups where the deviant was submissive.
3. The control technique (sending a person to the principal for talking) was rated as more fair by the classmates of submissive deviants.
4. More learning from the film took place in the groups in which the deviants responded submissively.

In general, the feelings of the witnesses seemed to parallel the feelings acted out by the deviant. The differences in learning give added weight to the importance of the deviant's response.

THE DEVIANT'S PRESTIGE

What happens to the ripple effect when a deviant is a leader? Are the effects the same when he has low prestige in his class? These questions were also researched in the "Miss Robe" experiment above. Two of the experimental classes watched a high-prestige deviant and two groups watched a low-prestige deviant perform. Their influence on the group had been measured previously by sociometric techniques.

Results showed that the ripple effect was significantly stronger when high-prestige deviants were involved than when low prestige culprits were disciplined. It is as though the bigger fish creates higher wavelets as he takes the bait.

WITNESS CHARACTERISTICS

Several members of Kounin's research team wanted to know whether there were any characteristics of the witnesses themselves that made them more or less susceptible to the influence from deviancy episodes. They were curious as to whether the ripple effects on some individuals differed from those on others.

In a study of high-school freshmen, Ofchus (1960) and Osborne (1961) established that: a deviancy episode is perceived much differently by students who are highly motivated to learn a subject than by their less interested classmates.

1. Highly motivated audiences rate deviancies as more disturbing and more serious.
2. Highly motivated students see control techniques as more fair and tend to take the teacher's side against deviants.
3. Students with low motivation perceived their teachers' control techniques as more angry, punitive, and approval-focused.
4. Highly motivated audiences react to a control technique by paying better attention to the learning task and behaving themselves in a more approved fashion.

These results also showed that "motivation to learn" and "liking for the teacher" were highly associated. When the effects were separated (Kounin, Gump, and Ryan, 1960) the following conclusions were reached:

1. One can predict ripple effects on audience attention and conformance by knowing the extent of their motivation to learn.
2. One can predict ripple effects on audience judgments about the control technique by knowing the extent of their liking for the teacher.

The nature of ripple effects, then, seems to be based on some characteristics of the audience students as well as those of the control techniques and the deviant.

Summary

The research cited in this chapter illustrates the importance of the deviancy episode in the discipline of the entire student group. It is evident that the teacher's interchange with each single deviant has important implications for his future success in control of classroom misbehavior. The following suggestions seem to be strongly indicated for any teacher who wishes to be an effective disciplinarian:

1. Locate and study the high-prestige students in your classes. As their responses to your influence have such a strong ripple

effect on the others, it will pay to find out which control techniques cause them to respond submissively with the least amount of belligerence.

2. Make use of nonthreatening techniques whenever possible. Since there are nearly always negative side effects associated with rough emotional handling, the total learning atmosphere will improve as the number of threats decreases.

3. Practice making your disciplinary commands clear and firm. If there is no doubt in your students' minds as to who the deviant is, what he is to stop, what he should do instead, and that you mean business, disciplinary problems become fewer with each passing day.

4. Make connections between your demands and the learning task at hand rather than to your own personal feelings.

5. Keep up with your field. When it becomes obvious that you are an expert in your subject matter, misbehavior is less frequent and more easily controlled.

6. Make your teaching as interesting as you possibly can. A "take it or leave it" attitude will only make deviancies more prevalent and more difficult to control.

7. Concentrating on being liked personally is less effective than concentrating on being an effective teacher where the classroom goals focus on optimum learning conditions.

References

Alden, E. *The Effects on Non-Target Classmates of the Teachers' Use of Expert Power and Liking Power in Controlling Deviant Behavior.* Doctor's thesis, Detroit, Wayne State University, 1959.

Gnagey, W. J. Effects on classmates of a deviant student's power and response to a teacher-exerted control technique. *Journal of Educational Psychology,* 1960, *51,* 1–9.

Kounin, J. S., and P. V. Gump. The ripple effect on discipline. *Elementary School Journal,* 1958, 59, 158–162.

Ofchus, L. T. *The Effects on Non-Target Classmates of Teachers' Efforts To Control Deviant Behavior.* Doctor's thesis, Detroit, Wayne State University, 1960.

Osborne, K. *Saliencies in Students' Perceptions of Teachers.* Doctor's thesis, Detroit, Wayne State University, 1961.

7

Classroom Discipline:
A Psychological Model

In the last six chapters we have tried to present a faithfully illustrated description of what research studies have told us about the control of misbehavior in the classroom. We have explained the role played in each disciplinary episode by the deviant, the teacher, the control technique, and the audience students. It is our belief that at this point the reader should have gained some understanding about the following topics:

1. Considerations that designate some behavior as misbehavior.
2. Forces that cause some students to become deviants.
3. Some teacher behaviors that increase the probability of a student's becoming deviant.
4. A number of antiseptic control techniques suitable for classroom use.
5. Ways that ripple effects may be used to increase a teacher's control of misbehavior.

In this chapter, we shall present a psychological model of classroom discipline that explains and organizes the foregoing material into a single set of applicable principles.

What Changes Student Behavior?

Behavior change is a familiar phenomenon to teachers. It is the primary reason they are in the classroom. They begin with pupils who are unable to write, read, add, or subtract. By the time they reach the twelfth grade, these same students can write poetry, read the classics, and solve problems using quadratic equations.

In order to accomplish this feat of behavior transformation, classroom experiences have to be arranged to follow a basic blueprint for human learning. It is our conviction that a good disciplinarian makes use of the same blueprint to teach acceptable deportment in the school classroom.

Briefly, a student learns to behave in ways that he believes either advance him toward his goals or protect him from harm. The feelings he experiences during the reward and punishment that accompany his behavior become associated with the persons and objects present when the feelings occur. These feelings and actions can later be triggered by persons and objects similar to those in the original situations.

The student of learning theory will recognize that this model leans heavily upon Neil Miller's (1941) conception of social learning.

A STUDENT'S GOALS

Each student has certain things he wants out of life. These are usually called goals or incentives. Some of these goals, such as food, water, and air, must be obtained just for the sake of physical survival. Because they are so important, they are often classified as basic or primary.

Some goals are learned from other people. The value that a student places upon school achievement, honesty, or cooperation is usually dependent upon the rewards and punishments he has experienced in the presence of others. As these goals are added on to the basic list and are not so crucial to physical survival, they are often called secondary needs or wants.

While students are about the business of obtaining what they want out of life, they become attached to the objects and people that are usually present when they reach their goals. Thus they have sentimental feelings about Mom's old silverware and Dad's old rocker, which were so often present when the students were gratifying their childhood needs. It is probable that their regard for Mom and Dad themselves is significantly enhanced by the fact that they were so instrumental in helping their children reach their primary and secondary goals for so many years.

Even persons and objects that resemble those present when

the students obtained their goals are valued as though they were the goals themselves. Although teachers like to take credit for the positive feelings that their students have for them, much of their "success" may be due to the fact that they are similar to parents who have already been associated with rewarding experiences.

THREATS TO A STUDENT.

Each student has certain things he wishes to stay away from. These are sometimes called negative goals or threats. Physical pain is one of the threats that the majority of students try to avoid. This is so common and has so many survival overtones that we might call pain a basic or primary threat. The children in Mrs. Stroud's class (Chapter 4) preferred even the stifling regimentation of a tyrant to the physical punishment she meted out.

Pupils also try to avoid situations that prevent them from reaching their goals. More than one high-school athlete has labored hard and long at his studies in order to avoid becoming ineligible for the team.

Feelings of fear and anxiety are such unpleasant threats that students will go to great lengths to avoid them. Feelings of fear are responses to anticipated pain or frustration. They are such powerful threats that most pupils will react to them long after the cause for the fear has vanished (Miller, 1948).

People and objects that have often been in close proximity to painful and unpleasant situations are avoided as though they themselves were threats. Even people and objects that resemble those present in threatening situations are avoided as though they could cause pain. It is not uncommon for some college students to go to almost any length to avoid taking even one unit of work in mathematics. Almost inevitably these feelings can be traced back to anxiety-laden courses in high school or elementary school.

CUES IN THE CLASSROOM

Being enamoured of certain goals and afraid of certain threats, students are always looking for more efficient means of getting what they want out of life. Any stimuli in the classroom that suggests more promising *modus operandi* are called cues. Cues not only indicate which way to act, but also when and where a profitable response might be made.

As a rich source of cues comes from other people in the classroom, imitation is at the base of a great many actions that students take (Miller and Dollard, 1941).

LEARNING TO REACH GOALS

Students learn to behave in ways that get them the things they want out of life (goals). When their actions help them to achieve these goals, they tend to repeat these behaviors under similar circumstances. Psychologists say that, because these successful responses bring pleasure, they are positively reinforced. The kindergarten lad who covets adult approval will learn to sit like a ramrod for the teacher who occasionally notes, "My, but I like the way Jimmie is sitting in his seat." But the disruptive antics of the classroom clown are also reinforced by the snickers of his appreciative classmates.

LEARNING TO AVOID THREATS

A pupil learns to behave in ways that allow him to avoid painful and fearful experiences. When he succeeds in circumventing these aversive situations, we say that his actions have been negatively reinforced. This means that they will likely be used again when danger appears on the horizon.

More than one student has learned to say, "I don't know," in preference to the humiliation he would suffer for making a mistake in front of the whole class. Truancy is another tragic example of one way that unsuccessful students seek to avoid the continual pain and frustration they experience at school.

Why Do Control Techniques Work?

As students seldom continue to behave in ways that fail to get them what they want (their goals) or protect them from what they wish to avoid (threats), there are four key questions a teacher must ask about a pupil who persistently misbehaves:

1. What goals and threats does he perceive in the classroom?
2. What are the classroom cues to which he is responding?
3. How are his deviant actions paying off?
4. How can approved behaviors be made to pay off more handsomely than deviancies?

In one way or another, the descriptive material presented in the earlier chapters falls rather neatly under one or more of these basic headings. By way of explanation, let us make a brief review of our findings using this new organization.

THEY CONTROL GOALS AND THREATS

In Chapter 2 it was explained that for moral, personal, legal, safety, and educational reasons, the classroom teacher, influenced by the community and school officials, makes certain definitions of acceptable and deviant behavior. In part, this means that he points out the goals and threats as he sees them. He reveals his perception of the consequences that should be sought after and those which should be specifically avoided.

Chapter 3 pointed out that deviancy may occur, either because the goals and threats pictured by the teacher are quite unlike the ones present in a student's home or neighborhood or because he sees nothing in the classroom that he wants.

The *absolute dictator* of Chapter 4 is accused of insisting upon his own goals without reference to those of his students. It is noted also that he institutes a comparatively large number of threats in his classes. In the same chapter, the *matinee idol* is charged with unwittingly allowing himself to become a goal of his student's romantic love. The *nonentity* is guilty of revealing no goals or threats at all and making his classroom an academic "guess-what."

The effectiveness of many of the control techniques described in Chapter 5 is due at least in part to the way the teacher handles the goal–threat situation with his students. In practicing *temptation removal,* a teacher rids the classroom of certain goals that seem antithetical to the education program at a given time. When *motivational recharging* is employed, new and inviting incentives are provided by the teacher in exchange for certain preferred learning behaviors.

The *practice alert* makes clear the goals and threats in a new situation which the students are about to enter, whereas *post mortem* sessions accomplish the same task after a deviancy has occurred.

Both *catharsis* and *comic relief* present release of tension buildup as an acceptable goal in the school situation.

Chapter 6 deals with what Miller and Dollard (1941) might call matched dependent behavior. It describes the way students behave after they witness a classmate's *modus operandi*. *Clarity* is effective partly because it makes the goals and threats in the situation more explicit to the deviant and the audience at the same time.

Although a *task-focused* technique emphasizes the connection between certain behaviors and the academic goals of the classroom, *approval-focused* techniques emphasize their relationship to some personal attachment to the teacher. Perhaps the comparative attractiveness of these two classes of goals depends on the balance of achievement and affiliation needs which a student brings into the situation (McClelland, *et al.*, 1953).

A *prestigeful deviant* is, by definition, a pupil whom many other pupils wish to copy. The goals that he tries to obtain are extremely attractive to those who identify with him. When their turn comes to take some action, many of the audience will try for the same incentives as their leader.

Highly motivated students are those who pursue the subject matter goals of the classroom. Their reactions to the teacher's control techniques tend to support the ones which facilitate the academic goals rather than the teacher-centered goals in the situation.

THEY MANIPULATE BEHAVIORAL CUES

Chapter 2 points out that in addition to controlling the goals and threats in the classroom, the teacher is responsible for giving cues concerning approved classroom deportment. Such cues may be in the form of an announced or published set of rules but may also be made clear by the way student behaviors are allowed to pay off.

Absence of clearly recognizable behavioral cues invites the kind of random trial and error that new teachers often experience during their first few weeks on the job. If this is interpreted as a plea for more cues instead of a subversive movement to overthrow the teacher's control, much needless anxiety can be averted. The teacher's energy can then be used in making the cues more explicit instead of concocting new kinds of defensive maneuvers.

Many deviants, as we pointed out in Chapter 3, have learned to operate in a home or neighborhood situation in which the cues have been markedly different from the typical school room. While aggression and violence were indicated in their out-of-school environment, they are definitely off limits in school. This means that some students must learn not to respond to cues that were meaningful in these other situations before they can respond to the new ones that are in the school environment. This initial frustration may cause feelings that produce other deviancies for some time until the cues are learned.

In Chapter 4, the *matinee idol* gives cues which call for amorous behavior on the part of his students. The *nonentity* emits no cues. A student must use a blind trial and error process, getting his cues from other students or some outside model. Often one student's trial responses may be incompatible with those of the others in his class.

Chapter 5 describes several control techniques that obtain part of their effectiveness from their influence upon the cues presented in the classroom. The use of *diagnostic pretests* is one way to find out to which cues a student is able to respond at the outset. The establishment of *routines* is merely an agreement about which behavioral responses are appropriate in response to certain standard cues.

In a *practice alert*, teachers make students aware beforehand of the important cues in a situation that will be new to them. *Post mortems* perform the same functions except that they are done after the fact.

If a teacher uses *catharsis* or *comic relief*, he presents cues which evoke responses that reduce emotional tension in the classroom.

When a teacher decides to *change the channel*, he begins to present some new and interesting cues in order to indicate an approach to the approved goals by a different route. Psychologists might term this a method of reducing reactive inhibition.

Visual prompting is an unobtrusive way of presenting cues to a deviant who is misbehaving.

One aspect of what we have called *restitution* consists of presenting cues to a deviant designed to elicit approved behavior immediately after he has broken a rule.

In a psychological analysis of the audience or *ripple effect* described in Chapter 6, we can categorize *clarity* partially as a method of making the behavioral cues obvious not only to the deviant, but also to the students who are watching the control technique. The responses of a high-prestige deviant furnish cues that illustrate to the audience one way of operating in the situation.

The *highly motivated* student will tend to react to cues that promise to help him move toward his academic goals. He judges each control technique on the information it gives him about this process. The *unmotivated* student tends to judge control techniques by the information they give him about the teacher.

THEY CONTROL REINFORCEMENT

The schedule of reinforcement in the classroom does not work in isolation from its other components. It is in the way that an action pays off, however, that exerts the most potent influence on student behavior. If a student acts out a forbidden behavior but is paid off by reaching one of his goals, he learns that this theoretically illegal action sometimes works. For the time being, this deviant has learned that crime *does* pay.

In like manner, any code-positive response that is followed by a punishment immediately becomes a threat by association. Just as the "proof of the pudding is in the eating," the proof of the appropriateness of a response is in the payoff. Even a momentary lapse in the consistency of the payoff program changes the classroom into a gambling device on which the student may make forbidden responses again and again hoping to hit the reinforcement jackpot on the next trial.

A deviant ceases to be a deviant only when he is convinced that the rules "on paper" are the actual rules by which the classroom pays off. As soon as he discovers the system and realizes that he can't beat it, his behavior begins to improve. Some psychologists would say that unreinforced deviancy becomes extinct when approved behaviors are reinforced.

A note of caution was injected in Chapter 3 when we were introduced to the *absolute dictator*. While he certainly ran a "tight ship" in terms of the consistency of the payoff program, the range of approved behaviors and goals was so narrow that some frustration resulted almost by definition. In this case, the in-class behavior may be quite acceptable, but the frustration-produced tensions are often vented upon innocent third parties outside the classroom.

The *matinee idol* who realizes what is going on and wishes deviants to stop trying for his romantic favors must monitor his own responses so that he never pays off for flirting.

As usual, the main trouble with the *nonentity* is that he refuses to exert any control over the payoffs whatsoever. This leaves the student to his own devices which are usually too immature to succeed.

A great number of control techniques owe their effectiveness to their influence upon the payoff pattern of the classroom. Whereas *ignoring* is a planned refusal to pay off anything for a certain deviancy, *retributive punishment* arranges for a painful payoff to suppress the forbidden behavior in the future.

A *practice alert* includes advance information about the payoffs in a new situation. Techniques which *make connections* point out the cause and effect relationships between certain actions and their payoff. *Post mortems* perform the same function after a deviancy has already occurred.

Comic relief and *catharsis* pay off in reduced tension which is built up during frustrating situations. In the use of *restitution,* a payoff is made for responding in an approved fashion immediately after a deviant action has been taken.

As the audience students watch a behavior pay off for someone they value, they often imitate his successful responses as they seek to reach their own goals. Whereas *clarity* calls attention to the way the deviant has misbehaved and points out the preferred actions in the situation, firmness is the procedure that keeps the system "honest." *Firmness* is the teacher making sure that the classroom situation pays off according to the rules he has enunciated.

Roughness refers to a painful payoff that is out of proportion to the magnitude of the deviancy. In their identification with the deviant, the audience feels unfairly punished by proxy. The learning situation then becomes a threat by association.

How Can This Psychology of Discipline Be Used?

Since our discipline model is based squarely upon learning principles, making plans to teach acceptable classroom behavior should follow the sequence used to plan any effective lesson.

MAKE BEHAVIORAL OBJECTIVES CLEAR AND SPECIFIC

Just as the good teacher begins an academic lesson plan with a list of aims, so must he spell out the kind of deportment he plans to teach. These goals should be as accepting as possible of individual differences within the framework of good educational practice. By taking time out to talk about each behavior sought, a teacher can make both the approved and prohibited outcomes clear and meaningful. Perhaps the most important function of making this list of aims is that it encourages the teacher to clear up in his own mind what behaviors he will seek to teach. Without making this decision it is impossible to maintain the consistency of reinforcement that is vital to the process.

IMPROVE THE QUALITY OF BEHAVIORAL CUES

As Jerome Kagan (1967) has recently pointed out, the distinctiveness of cues in a situation may well be the most important influence in the learning process. Although some cues may come from objects, most come from the persons in the classroom situations. This not only means that a teacher must practice what he preaches, but that the sooner he improves the deportment of the leaders in the classroom, the sooner others who take their cues from them will shape up. Certainly any control technique a teacher uses must begin with a cue that is clearly discriminable from the other stimuli in the room at the time.

GIVE AND WITHHOLD REINFORCEMENT

Perhaps the *sine qua non* of effective teaching concerns one's ability to reinforce desired behavior and keep undesirable responses from being rewarded. While this has been quite widely accepted in the teaching of academic material, its application to classroom behavior problems has been sparse.

One reason for this failure may be the widespread acceptance of punishment as an antidote for deviancy. There are few teachers who would paddle a student for failing a history test. Let him make such a failure in deportment, however, and punishment is almost sure to follow. The destructive effects of retributive punishment have been discussed in Chapter 5.

In Chapter 8 we shall present a number of recent case histories that illustrate the powerful influence that systematic use of reinforcement can have on the discipline in the classroom. These illustrations are all drawn from research accounts of carefully planned efforts to change deviant behavior.

References

Kagan, J. On the need for relativism. *American Psychologist*, 1967, 22, 131–142.

McCelland, D. C., J. W. Atkinson, R. A. Clark, and R. A. Lowell. *The Achievement Motive*. New York. Appleton-Century-Crofts, 1953.

Miller, N. E. Studies of fear as an acquirable drive: I. Fear as a motivation and fear-reduction as reinforcement in the learning of new responses. *Journal of Experimental Psychology*, 1948, 38, 89–101.

Miller, N. E., and J. Dollard. *Social Learning and Imitation*. New Haven. Yale, 1941.

Ullman, L., and L. Krasner. *Case Studies in Behavior Modification*. New York. Holt, Rinehart and Winston, 1965.

8

Case Studies: Applying the Model

In the last chapter we demonstrated how the results of a long list of discipline research studies could be organized under a few postulates of learning. This not only allows us to see the underlying similarities among several diverse approaches to the problem, but it becomes a bridge to another small, but growing body of research: human behavior control. In this chapter we will present some brief descriptions of classrooms in which a systematic application of a psychological learning model improved the discipline markedly. Although none of the situations will be exactly like those in the reader's experience, certain parallels will become obvious.

ELIMINATING CLASSROOM TANTRUMS

Zimmerman and Zimmerman (1962) describe an emotionally upset lad of eleven who threw a kicking and screaming tantrum several times a week. Whenever he was brought to his classroom, he would throw himself down in front of the door and being the histrionics. This usually drew a crowd of staff members who stood around him to witness the spectacle and comment on the probable causes of his misbehavior.

The teacher, sensing that the crowding around of staff members might be rewarding the tantrum behavior, had the lad brought into the classroom and placed in his seat. Although the boy kept kicking and screaming, his teacher went about her own work ignoring his outbursts. After two or three minutes, his tantrum had subsided and the youngster looked up at his teacher.

Taking advantage of his momentary attentiveness, his teacher told him that she would begin his lesson whenever he was ready. At this, the distraught lad began to cry and scream again. This outburst lasted for about five minutes. Then he sat up and said he was ready to begin.

His teacher immediately looked up at him and smiled. She walked over to his desk and said, "Good, now let's get to work." For the rest of that class period, this eleven-year-old worked quietly and cooperatively at his lessons.

During the days that followed, this teacher stuck to a well-planned system of withholding and giving reinforcement. Whenever her unruly pupil threw another tantrum, she assiduously ignored him. Whenever he quieted down, she came over closer to him, talked with him, or began an activity that she knew he liked. After several weeks under the new system, the boy's classroom tantrums stopped altogether.

Although his tantrums had been eliminated, this youngster continued to do other things that upset the learning situation. Not only did he use baby talk in class, but he constantly broke in with completely irrelevant comments and questions.

Following the same system that had vanquished the tantrums, his teacher paid absolutely no attention to either the baby talk or his inappropriate comments and questions. But whenever the lad was working quietly or making an acceptable contribution to class, she would talk with him pleasantly or ask him a question she was sure he could answer.

As with the tantrums, this lad's disruptive verbal behavior almost completely disappeared. He was able to work more efficiently in his classroom and was making good progress at the end of the study.

ANALYSIS

1. *What were some goals and threats that this lad perceived in the classroom?* His teacher hypothesized that if a crowd of staff members served to reward his tantrum behavior, a probable goal for him was adult concern, affection, or approval. Perhaps the classroom was a threat, because the youngster was forced to share the teacher with several other classmates.

2. *To what cues was this eleven-year-old responding?* The Zimmermans' description does not tell us how the boy hit upon tantrum behavior as a method of securing adult attention. He might have easily seen it pay off for another child. It is also possible that he accidentally stumbled upon the strategy when copious amounts of adult concern followed a period of raw emotional release.

It seemed apparent to his teacher, however, that he was sensitive to the responses of the adults around him. The first time the youngster was receptive, she gave him a clear indication of how he was to behave in class. When he refused to take the cue and continued his tantrum behavior, she was firm and followed through on her promise that the lesson would begin only when he was ready.

3. *How were the boy's tantrums paying off?* In this particular case, the unruly behavior was certainly receiving adult concern. It also may have been useful in avoiding threats in the classroom situation. It does not appear to have been pure emotional release in this case, though the Zimmermans did note that some tantrum behavior persisted in other nonclassroom situations.

4. *How was approved behavior made to pay off more handsomely than deviancy?* As far as the teachers were concerned, affectionate responses were withheld for all except nondeviant behaviors. Tantrums, baby talk and irrelevant verbalizations gained nothing except the teacher's stony indifference. The disruptive behaviors became extinct because they were no longer tools for obtaining adult concern. The frequency of constructive classroom behavior increased, because it was the only method by which adult concern rewards could be obtained.

CONTROLLING MISBEHAVIOR IN A NURSERY SCHOOL

L. E. Homme and his associates (1963) describe the exquisite pandemonium of the first day of a nursery school when no threats or punishments were used to keep order. The teacher's instructions to "sit down" had almost no effect on the gleeful, running, screaming, chair-pushing, puzzle-working preschool youngsters.

Acting upon the suggestion of another reasearcher (Premack, 1959), Homme's group took careful note of the favorite, high-probability behaviors performed by these children in an uninhibiting setting. As all experienced nursery-school teachers know, traditional school behaviors, such as sitting quietly and looking at the board, are very low-probability responses initially.

In order to increase the frequency of constructive classroom behavior, favorite, high-probability behaviors were used as rewards. One method was to signal a "running and screaming" time after a period of quiet attentiveness to a lesson.

Later children could earn tokens for proper (but low-frequency) behavior. These could subsequently be used to buy time for doing favorite (high-probability) behaviors.

After a few days, Homme and his coworkers were amazed at the near-perfect control that the teacher had achieved. The experimenters also noted that in a typical school, most of the favorite behaviors of these children would have been suppressed by one kind of punishment or another.

ANALYSIS

1. *What goals or threats did these children perceive in the nursery school?* Although some psychologists would say that they were motivated by "muscle hunger" or an activity need, the Homme group was content to note that they preferred some activities over others. They also found that many other preferred activities could be found with a little experimentation. The usual threats were not present in this classroom.

2. *To what cues were they responding?* Although there was undoubtedly a great deal of imitation going on that first day, the running, screaming, chair-pushing, puzzle-working behavior is not atypical of children of this age in other situations. Perhaps the most important fact in this classroom was that the youngsters were *not* responding to the teacher's directions.

Later on, bells were used as signals for the "running and screaming fun" which followed the quiet attentive periods. The teacher's verbal instructions became important because following her suggestions paid off.

3. *How were the initial, high-frequency, disruptive responses paying off?* The Homme group avoided this question, but one assumption implicit in their system seems to be: high-probability behavior is more reinforcing than low-probability behavior. In

other words, children do fun things with greater frequency than non-fun things in a free choice situation.

In a sort of postscript, these researchers reported that cup-throwing, wastebasket-kicking, and giving the experimenter a ride on a caster-equipped chair, all proved to be highly reinforcing even though they were not observed on the first day. This would support the idea that a child's personal goals and threats may not show up without some study on the teacher's part.

4. *How were approved behaviors made to pay off?* Perhaps the genius of this experiment lies in the use of "deviant" behaviors to reinforce nondeviant actions. Of course, none of the "deviant" behaviors was really dangerous (even the cups they threw were plastic), although they would most certainly have to be outlawed for educational reasons. Although "deviant" behaviors still paid off because they were "fun," they were planned for at special times and thereby kept from interfering with quiet learning activities.

Twenty-seven Aggressive Boys Become Peaceful

Brown and Elliott (1965) set out to change the aggressive behavior of 27 three- and four-year-olds in a nursery-school situation. Trained raters watched the children during a daily 1-hour free play period and marked down every time any boy was verbally or physically aggressive.

Such acts as pushing, pulling, holding, hitting, annoying, teasing, interfering, disparaging, and threatening were all recorded for a week to get an idea of the level of aggression before the experiment began. There was an average of 64 aggressive acts per hour of free play during those first five days.

Two weeks later, the nursery-school teachers were asked to try a new approach. They were to stoically ignore all aggressive acts (if they weren't really dangerous) and reward only cooperative and peaceful behavior. These rewards were to take the form of a friendly pat on the head, saying "that's good," greeting children cordially, drawing attention to something a child had made, etc. At the same time teachers were asked not to make any aggressive boys say they were sorry or use any kind of punishment.

Brown and Elliott noted that it seemed very hard for the nursery-school teachers to ignore aggression. In the beginning, they weren't at all convinced that the new approach would succeed and often caught themselves moving in on a fight without thinking. With help from the experimenter, these women were soon able to maintain free play periods in which peace was rewarded and war was ignored. This sort of diplomacy was maintained for two weeks. Whereas there had been an average of 64 aggressive acts per hour before the treatment began, there were only 43 per hour during the 10-day treatment period.

At this point the teachers were told that the experiment was over and they could do what they wanted to about aggressive acts. Three weeks later the raters came back again to see if the gains that had been made were holding up. They recorded an average of 52 aggressive acts per hour, showing that the boys had slipped back into some of their old pugnacious habits, but not all the way back.

Two weeks after the check-up rating were completed, the teachers agreed to try two more weeks of ignoring aggression and rewarding peaceful coexistence. Ratings made during the last week showed that these formerly warlike little lads were now committing an average of only 26 aggressive acts per hour and, as with all other tabluations, this included all 27 three- and four-year-old boys!

Not only were these teachers convinced of the success of this method, but they were openly astounded at the unexpected increase of friendly, cooperative responses of the two most troublesome youngsters in the group.

ANALYSIS

1. *What goals and threats did these aggressive boys see in nursery school?* Brown and Elliott thought that most of these children were seeking adult attention. Ever since their birth, an attending adult had been present when their basic goals were reached. It is probable that at ages three and four, adult attention is sought as though it were a goal in its own right. Although threats from other children and disapproving teachers were certainly part of the situation, the threat of loss of adult attention was probably quite strong.

2. *What were the cues to which these youngsters were*

responding? Cues from other children could certainly have caused some of the aggressive behavior to spread. The outcome of the experiment, however, showed that cues given by the teachers were probably more effective. Because of their recent complete dependence, nursery school children seem maximally sensitive to cues from adults.

3. *How were the boys' deviancies paying off?* In the usual school setup, aggression commandeers adult attention like nothing else a boy can do. It seems evident that these youngsters were using aggressive acts as tools to focus a larger share of the teacher's attention upon them. Some "fighting back" certainly defended the boys against the threats of their attackers, but in the end, this seemed less consequential than it might at first appear.

4. *How were peaceful behaviors made to pay off more handsomely than warlike behaviors?* Although suppressing a "natural urge" to break up fights and punish aggressive acts, these teachers soon gave all the social rewards to children who were cooperative and made aggressiveness a waste of time as far as garnering adult attention was concerned.

Improving Discipline in Five Elementary Classes

Becker and his associate (1967) describe an experiment in which two deviant children from each of five classrooms in an elementary school were chosen as targets for improvement. Two six-year-olds were chosen from a lower-primary class of 23; two nine-year-olds from one lower-intermediate class of 26; two ten-year-olds from a second lower-intermediate class of 25; two seven-year-olds from one middle-primary room; and one seven- and one eight-year-old from a second middle-primary class of 20.

For five weeks, specially trained observers tabulated the deviant and relevant (acceptable) behaviors of the target children in order to establish the rate of deviancy before the experimental treatment began. On the average, 62 per cent of their actions were deviant during this initial period.

During the next nine weeks, all teachers were to follow several basic rules in classroom management. These rules were typed on a 5 × 8-inch card and kept on their desks!

1. Make rules for each period explicit as to what is expected of children. (Remind them of rules when needed.)
2. *Ignore* (do not attend to) behaviors which interfere with learning or teaching, unless a child is being hurt by another. Use punishment which seems appropriate, preferably withdrawal of some positive reinforcement.
3. Give *praise* and *attention* to behaviors which facilitate learning. Tell child what he is being praised for. Try to reinforce behaviors incompatible with those you wish to decrease. (At this point several examples of how to praise were listed.) In general, give praise for achievement, prosocial behavior, and following group rules.

The experimental teachers agreed to participate in a workshop and seminar to assist them in applying the rules printed on the card. During the experiment the teachers' behaviors were also rated to make sure that the rules were being followed.

When deviant and acceptable behaviors of the target students were tabulated at the end of the nine-week treatment period, the average proportion of deviancies had dropped to 29 per cent as compared to the 62 per cent computed for the base-line period.

The Becker group went on to describe in some detail the background, behavior changes, and reactions of both the target students and their teachers to this "new approach." They concluded that many different kinds of teachers could learn to apply the rules successfully in classrooms with normal pupil-teacher ratios.

ANALYSIS

1. What goals and threats did these ten children perceive in their classrooms? The strength of this experiment is that it allows the establishment of different goals in each classroom, depending upon the predilection of the teacher and the ability of the student. In two of Becker's classes, special instructions were given for deviants with unusual problems, but they always conformed to the basic rules printed on the card. Many of the usual threats were removed when punishment was replaced by ignoring.

2. What were the classroom cues to which these students

were responding? This study ignores almost all but those supplied by the teacher. The very first rule emphasizes the importance of a clear, precise description of what is expected during each school period. Rule 1 also directs the teacher to remind students of the expectations when necessary.

3. *How were their deviant actions paying off?* Here again, the assumption was that teacher-attention was reinforcing deviant actions. Every time that some deviancy procured an extra share of the teacher's time, the deviant was rewarded for his misbehavior.

4. *How were the approval (relevant) behaviors made to pay off more handsomely than deviant behaviors?* Rules 2 and 3 on the printed card spelled out these procedures. When interfering behaviors are ignored, they no longer pay off in teacher attention. Simultaneously, facilitating behaviors became the only way to gain friendly interaction with the adult in the situation.

Becker's data suggest that this approach is less effective for children who fall into one or more of three categories: those for whom the school work is too difficult; those whose deviancies are reinforced by their classmates; and those whose deviancies are so frequent that they very seldom make a response that can be reinforced.

A Unique Solution to a Serious Problem

O'Leary and Becker (1967) describe a successful "token reinforcement" program that they set up in a third-grade "adjustment" class. The class was made up of 17 nine-year-old children who were placed in this class because of their disruptive antics in the regular classroom. According to reports, temper tantrums, crying, fighting, and uncontrolled laughter were all reasons for sending these children to the "adjustment" class.

Previous experience had convinced the psychologists that such standard school rewards as praise, teacher attention, or stars or grades would not work with this class. One of their regular teachers insisted that when she called them "bad," they seemed to take it as a compliment and stepped up their rate of deviancy. When she complimented them on having done something well, they seemed disappointed and made faces at each other.

Using carefully trained observers, O'Leary and Becker recorded the behavior of the 8 most deviant children for four weeks in advance of the experimental treatment. These third-graders were observed while they were participating in three structured activities: group reading, arithmetic, and listening to records or stories. A partial list of the behaviors marked as deviant included pushing, answering without raising one's hand, chewing gum, eating, name-calling, and talking and making other disruptive noises.

During the four weeks prior to the treatment, the average proportion of deviant behavior for all the observed children was 76 per cent. The daily means of deviant behavior ranged from 66 to 91 per cent.

The next step in this experiment was to institute a carefully planned system for decreasing the proportion of deviant behavior and increasing the relative frequency of acceptable classroom behavior. Six simple instructions were placed on the board at the beginning of each day of the first week. They were: In Seat, Face Front, Raise Hand, Working, Pay Attention, and Desk Clear. The point system was then carefully explained to the entire class.

The children were informed that they would receive a certain number of points in their book, depending on how well they followed the instructions on the board. These points could later be used to "buy" small prizes such as candy, pennants, comics, perfume, and kites. A large variety of these "backup reinforcers" made it more probable that every child could find something that he wished to spend his points on.

At first, the points were given at the end of each lesson period about five times a day. Initially, the teacher didn't want to go along with the rating procedure, because she thought it would take up too much time. When she found that she could give out all the points in three minutes, she agreed to try it.

For the first three days, points could be exchanged for prizes immediately after the token periods. During the next four days the children had to save up points for two days before they could spend them. The number of saving days was gradually increased so that during the last twenty-four school days, the children had to save up points for four days before they were allowed to buy prizes.

In order to make traditional social rewards more useful, the teacher was trained to give praise that was associated with prizes. She would often say, "I am glad to see everyone turned around in their seats. That will help all of you get the prize you want." The teacher also was instructed to ignore the deviant behavior of one child while rewarding another close child for obeying the same rule.

While the teacher was marking the individual points in each child's book, the group was usually directed by an appointed classmate who asked individuals to read portions of a story that had been placed on the board. Group points were added to a thermometer chart in the back of the room depending on how well the whole class behaved during the individual rating period. After a certain number of group points were accumulated, popsicles were given to all 17 children.

Expert observers once more recorded time samples of the same children's behavior during the two months when the point system was in effect. An unbelievably low 10 per cent of the recorded behaviors were rated as deviant during that experimental period, while 76 per cent had been observed during the base period before the treatment began.

In addition, as so little of the teacher's time was taken up with discipline, she was able to give each child much more individual attention and had time to correct papers so that they could be returned quickly. According to O'Leary and Becker, the learning situation was so vastly improved that some children who had not finished an assignment for two years began to get perfect papers for the first time.

ANALYSIS

1. What goals and threats had these third-graders perceived in their regular classes? Because being "bad" seemed to be preferred to being "good," the least we can say is that those third-graders had different goals in mind than would usually be assumed for third-graders. It is possible that their constant misbehavior defended them against the failure they believed would result from taking the academic work seriously.

With the institution of the point system, goals such as candy, comics and perfume were introduced into the classroom. Suddenly there was something at school that they wanted.

2. *What were the classroom cues to which these deviants were responding?* There is some evidence that these nine-year-olds were using the teacher's cues as signals to perform the opposite of what she had intended.

At the beginning of the "point system," some new behavioral cues were put on the board in terms that could not be mistaken. As a misbehaving child was ignored, it seemed useless to adopt his antics as a cue to imitate. Both deviants and audience children saw that behaving got both primary and secondary rewards and took their cues from these events.

3. *How were their deviant actions paying off in the regular classrooms?* Perhaps, as in some other cases, deviancy was the most effective way to command coveted adult attention. It seems probable from the account that some group prestige was gained by being labeled "bad." If these third-graders had experienced a lot of failures in academic areas, unruly behavior not only accorded them a certain notoriety not possible for them in their usual lessons, but it may also have protected them from the ignominy of experiencing new failures.

4. *How were the approved behaviors made to pay off more handsomely than deviant behaviors?* With attractive goals introduced into the school situation, following instructions suddenly began to pay off in tangible goods. Deviancies were ignored, and they no longer procured the perverse satisfaction that had once reinforced them. It became as clear as the instructions on the board that if he wanted to get in on the goodies, a pupil's behavior would have to change.

By gradual increases of the intervals between buying times, waiting or patience was rewarded. Using our principle that stimuli which are present when reinforcement takes place become reinforcers themselves, O'Leary and Becker paired the point system with the more usual rewards of praise and adult attention. In this way, social rewards that at first did not work with these children began to gain in reinforcing strength.

How Will You Apply the Model?

If you are an experienced teacher, you may have responded to some of the foregoing descriptions with the thought, "But I've done that for years." Certainly you have, if you have been successful. After a certain number of trials and errors, most of us catch on to some system that works for us in our situation. There are two advantages that most of these experiments have over the usual learn-by-experience method: analysis and system.

CAREFUL ANALYSIS

In each of the five case studies presented, some thoughtful person or group sat down and made a determined attempt to answer the "goals, cues, and payoff" questions that we have reiterated in this chapter. Unlike many dictionary drills and workbook exercises, the answers are not always the same. Your own particular classroom must be analyzed for its own unique answers. Some of these answers may indicate methods and rewards that are so unusual that some personal bravery is demanded on your part in order to put them into effect.

FOLLOWING A SYSTEM

Researchers like the ones cited throughout this chapter are noted for their systematic approach. Sometimes the main difference between an experimental treatment and a classroom policy is that the former is consistently carried out in the prescribed manner, whereas the latter remains relatively hit or miss. Although this certainly has "firmness" implications, it also suggests differences in planning. As with good academic learning experiences, good disciplinary procedures owe much of their success to careful planning.

BEING EXPERIMENTAL

Experimentation suggests at least two directions in which a good disciplinarian should move: toward innovation and toward more adequate measurement.

Innovation is almost a cliché in modern educational circles. Some psychologists insist that making some changes in a learning situation may be much more important than the specific kind of changes you make (Kagan, 1967). At any rate, teachers are always trying something new to spark their academic efforts.

But innovations are also sorely needed in classroom discipline.

For some reason creativity has been sadly lacking when it comes to handling the deviant. One such challenge lies in the controlling of deviancy among high-school students who do not respond to the traditional middle-class social rewards. You may have noticed that none of the case studies involved high-school classes. One reason is certainly the fact that adult approval and praise have become less important for the adolescent whereas peer approval has become the major reinforcer.

Would you be brave enough to suggest that "group deportment points" could be given to an unruly sophomore English class to save up for a free sock hop with a local musical "group"? Would coed picnics and parties work? Would something else appeal more to your sophomore?

If you were teaching in a "blackboard jungle" class, would you be willing to *pay* high-school students to work and learn? If they could purchase the things they wanted out of life by working at their schooling, would their resulting education open up new possibilities for them? Is it possible that education would become more rewarding itself because of its obvious connection to buying power? Is being paid for doing schoolwork inconsistent with the way our society operates? Would paying these deprived students to work and learn be any more expensive than some of the other remedial programs in which we are now engaged?

Adequate measurement has been a traditional part of teacher education for many years. The techniques of making and interpreting subject matter tests are usually covered in the courses required for obtaining a teacher's certificate.

But very little instruction is ever given in the objective evaluation of disciplinary improvement. Who gives pretests in deportment? What data do you have to support your *feeling* that classroom deviancy is getting better or worse?

You will remember that, in most of the case histories, a deviancy measure was conducted during a base period preceding the experimental approach. Could you devise a check list to use before and after your disciplinary innovations? Would your supervisor help? Would it be rewarding to you to see your own discipline improve?

References

Becker, W. C., C. H. Madsen, C. R. Arnold, and D. R. Thomas. *The Contingent Use of Teacher Attention and Praise in Reducing Classroom Behavior Problems.* Paper presented at AERA, New York, February, 1967.

Brown, P., and R. Elliott. Control of aggression in a nursery school class. *Journal of Experimental Child Psychology,* 1965, *2,* 103–107.

Homme, L. E., P. C. deBaca, J. V. Devine, R. Steinhorst, and E. J. Rickert. Use of the Premack principle in controlling the behavior of nursery school children. *Journal of the Experimental Analysis of Behavior,* 1963, *6,* 544.

Kagan, J. On the need for relativism. *American Psychologist,* 1967, *22,* 131–142.

O'Leary, K. D., and W. C. Becker. Behavior modification of an adjustment class: A token reinforcement program. *Exceptional Children,* 1967, *33,* 637–642.

Premack, D. Toward empirical behavior laws: I. Positive reinforcement. *Psychological Review,* 1959, *66,* 219–233.

Zimmerman, E. H., and J. Zimmerman. The alteration of behavior in a special classroom situation. *Journal of the Experimental Analysis of Behavior,* 1962, *5,* 59–60.

4183